The Etch-a-Sketch

and Other Fun Programs

Brian Wiser

Produced by:
Brian Wiser & Bill Martens

Apple PugetSound Program Library Exchange

The ETCH-A-SKETCH and Other Fun Programs

ACKNOWLEDGEMENTS

The Etch-a-Sketch and Other Fun Programs were programmed by Brian Wiser and are Copyright 2019-2022 © Brian Wiser. All stories and chapters in this book and Wiser's personal photos and art are copyright © 2019-2022 Brian Wiser. All rights reserved.

This book, produced by Brian Wiser and released with his permission, is copyright by A.P.P.L.E. as the publisher. No claim to copyright is created outside of those portions created by A.P.P.L.E..

Special thanks to Lane Roathe and Bill Martens for programming advice.

The Cover, Art, and Book were designed by Brian Wiser.

PRODUCTION

Brian Wiser → Design, Layout, Editing, Preface, Programming
Bill Martens → Disk Updates

DISCLAIMER

ABOUT BRIAN WISER

Brian Wiser is a producer of books, films, games, and events, as well as a long-time consultant, enthusiast and historian of Apple, the Apple II and Macintosh. Steve Wozniak and Steve Jobs, as well as *Creative Computing*, *Nibble*, *InCider*, and *A+* magazines were early influences.

Brian designed, edited, and co-produced dozens of books including: *Nibble Viewpoints: Business Insights From The Computing Revolution, Cyber Jack: The Adventures of Robert Clardy and Synergistic Software, Synergistic Software: The Early Games, The Colossal Computer Cartoon Book: Enhanced Edition, All About Applesoft: Enhanced Edition, Graphically Speaking: Enhanced Edition, What's Where in the Apple: Enhanced Edition*, and *The WOZPAK: Special Edition* – an important Apple II historical book with Steve Wozniak's restored original, technical handwritten notes. Brian is also the author of *The Etch-a-Sketch and Other Fun Programs*.

He passionately preserves and archives all facets of Apple's history, and noteworthy companies such as Beagle Bros and Applied Engineering, featured on AppleArchives.com. His writing, interviews and books are featured on the technology news site CallApple.org and in *Call-A.P.P.L.E.* magazine that he co-produces as an A.P.P.L.E. board member. Brian also co-produced the retro iOS game *Structris*.

In 2005, Brian was cast as an extra in Joss Whedon's movie *Serenity*, leading him to being a producer and director for the documentary film *Done The Impossible: The Fans' Tale of Firefly & Serenity*. He brought some of the *Firefly* cast aboard his Browncoat Cruise convention and recruited several of the *Firefly* cast to appear in a film for charity. Throughout these experiences, he develops close personal relationships with many actors, authors, and computer industry luminaries. Brian speaks about his adventures to large audiences at conventions around the country.

 I would like to dedicate this book to my computer teacher and friend, Richard Siddoway. My life was never the same after learning from you and exploring with you the possibilities that technology brought us.

CONTENTS

Preface..vii

Graphics

The Etch-a-Sketch 1

The Apple 17

Motherboard Simulation 19

Lo-Res Horizontal Line... 29

Education

Annual Graph Matrix 31

Compound Interest 33

States & Capitals.. 35

Utilities

Access Code 39

H 41

Random Access Filer 45

Games

Tunnel Race 51

The Autobahn.. 55

Joystick Calibration... 61

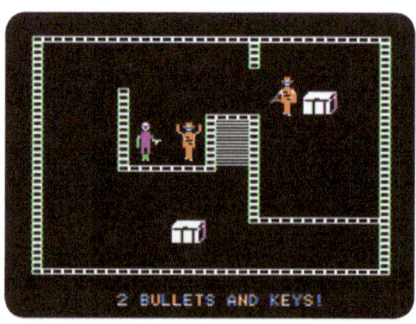

Castle Wolfenstein (Muse Software, 1981)

Marauder (Sierra On-Line, 1982)

PREFACE

The 1980s. For me, it was the golden age of discovering all the possibilities that computers had and could bring, courtesy of my first computer – an Apple II Plus. My dad's work was upgrading their computers and sent him home with a 48K Apple II Plus, two 5.25" Disk II drives, Zenith monitor, Apple joystick, and a box of mystery disks. One of the disks contained *Castle Wolfenstein* and *Marauder*! I was transported to another world, never to return. Not bad for a free computer system that I miraculously still have.

After indulging my senses every day playing these new games, I wanted to learn how to program my Apple II and make it do even more. My dad gave me David Ahl's *Basic Computer Games* – the rare yellow cover version with the cute robots. I had fun typing the BASIC programs and imagining what could be created, but I grew frustrated that so much of what was accurately typed did not completely work. It was confusing and disheartening, and I had no Apple manuals to refer to. In frustration, I threw the book away.

Sometime later, I took my first formal programming classes in high school and learned that BASIC varied from computer to computer. So that's why those programs didn't work! At last I had an answer that made me feel better about the challenges of programming. Knowledge had begun, but I regretted the impulse of throwing away that book.

Years later, I longed to have my first programming book and was unable to find that version. The universe must have forgiven me, because Robert Clardy of Synergistic Software bestowed upon me his personal copy when we met to collaborate on his *Cyber Jack* autobiography. At last, I had my programming book again! It was even more special having been part of Robert's programming foundation and ultimately his company that published so many important programs.

Apple IIe computer lab with Brian and friends

Unlike today, computer programming was taught in school and it was a requirement. I fully embraced that requirement in a class called "Data Processing," spending a year learning Applesoft BASIC on the Apple IIe. The class touched on many concepts and engendered a new way of thinking about the world.

Learning these concepts and fulfilling class assignments, I wrote tools like: *Annual Graph Matrix*, *Compound Interest*, *Random Access Filer*, and *States & Capitals*. I learned a little bit about low-resolution graphics writing *The Apple*, which was a simple representation of the Apple Computer logo and an expression of my genuine love for Steve Wozniak's invention. And I learned a bit about high-resolution graphics writing a racing game called *The Autobahn*.

Being passionate about graphics, my so-called programming crowning achievement was a tool that I dubbed *The Etch-a-Sketch*. I had fun imaging all the things I could do with it, like adding sound and joystick control to an otherwise simple drawing program. And I took all of that fun into many of my other classes and breaks, writing BASIC code in a notebook over many months. Eventually, the program grew to about 18K in size.

I used the Beagle Bros program *GPLE* by Neil Konzen, that helped me fit more code on a single line in BASIC than was otherwise possible. Beagle Bros software was some of the only software I purchased with my hard-earned money. They had a unique spirit of fun and exploration throughout their valuable programs, advertisements, and newsletters. That spirit was catching.

I'll never forget when my teacher Richard Siddoway excitedly announced to the class that, "Brian has exploded his *Etch-a-Sketch*" and asked me to demonstrate it. That explosion was enlarged a bit, as my demo and all of his tutorials were done on a 40-inch TV connected to an Apple IIe! Having had such a positive experience with a teacher who genuinely cared and encouraged his students furthered my computer passions.

Mr. Siddoway also worked alongside students in the lab, which included the IBM 5150 in addition to Apple IIe systems. It was clear that he was just as fascinated with computers and eager to expand his skills. And more importantly, this erased some of the traditional boundaries between teachers and students – he was one of us.

Richard Siddoway programming on an IBM 5150

The second year of Data Processing was optional, but of course I wanted more training. I even convinced the other teacher to hold an Apple II machine language class – with me as the only student. Still to this day, I remain impressed and grateful that he took that extra time to make me happy. I learned how to count in binary and write some simple machine language programs. Ironically, the school had no assembly language editors, so I found a copy of the *Big Mac* assembler published by the A.P.P.L.E. user group and used that to program with. It's ironic that years later, among the books I designed as part of A.P.P.L.E. is a new compilation of the *Big Mac* manuals.

The final exam was to draw a high-resolution picture partially peeking through a small window, with keys to move around. My theme, not surprisingly, was a simplified Apple IIe logic board as seen in the *Motherboard Simulation*. This assignment was anything but simple to complete. Where the BASIC programming language is more readable and approachable (`10 PRINT "Hello World"`), machine language references areas in the computer's memory displayed in hexadecimal and uses three-letter commands (`6D06: STX $78E`). Machine language is the native programming language of a computer, so it runs faster than BASIC.

Beyond formal classes, I always stayed after school with my friends for our anything-goes computer club that someone dubbed "The Bad Apples." We mostly programmed and played popular games like *Cannonball Blitz, Lode Runner, Bilestoad*, and *Ultima IV*. I also enjoyed *The Ancient Art of War* on the IBM 5150! Occasionally, we even had a school-funded pizza party. Why go home and play with my new, souped-up Apple IIe when I had so many friends to share this crazy passion with?

Alas, that Apple IIe was sold at some point to fund my Apple IIGS purchase. That's indeed a tragedy, as I had an RGB card and an expensive Panasonic monitor that gave me the ability to choose a text color like amber, instead of the traditional green. It also contained various Applied Engineering cards and a Thirdware Fingerprint card for printing and saving screens via a simple touch.

Of course, I enjoyed the world of BBS's (Bulletin Board Systems) with my Prometheus ProModem 2400 and connected my computer to another in the world before the Internet – posting public messages, exchanging email, and playing games.

My friends and fellow Bad Apples trying to look sophisticated

Along the way at the computer club, I started modifying and improving programs that I came across. One such program was a startup program called "*H*" that simplified launching programs with a single key in DOS 3.3. I converted the text to title case, updated the design, and added additional features. Another discovered program was a text-based game called *Tunnel Race* that illustrated the landscape with keyboard characters, and I made similar enhancements to that. I never knew who originally wrote those programs, but I enjoyed having another avenue to practice programming and enhancement techniques.

The purpose of this book is twofold. First, it serves as a nice nostalgic memory and allows me to revisit these programs and experiences with my friends. And more importantly, it offers a glimpse into concepts that were taught and hopefully provides some practical enjoyment for enthusiasts and programmers. If you use any of my routines in your own programs, please acknowledge the authorship of those routines in your program. Most of my programs are included in this book and can be downloaded on a disk image from: www.callapple.org/books.

Speaking of enjoyment, there was an especially amusing incident at our school's computer club that I'll never forget. One of my friends saved a hi-res screen from a game he bought, and was playing with that graphic. A teacher saw the game screen and, thinking it was an illegal copy of the game, asked to see the disk. My friend explained how he extracted the picture from his original disk at home, but the teacher refused to believe him.

In moments, they were both clutching the 5.25" disk drive, as the teacher was struggling to get the disk out, and my friend was trying to keep the disk in. Suddenly, I was watching a wrestling match with both of them and the disk drive hitting the floor along with the Apple IIe! I don't remember what finally convinced the teacher, perhaps the determination and truthfulness of my friend, but the teacher apologized and replaced the destroyed disk. Passion for original software I suppose, or copy protection in action?

Although I never considered myself a programmer, certainly not by today's standards, I did have some skill. Those high school classes and *especially* Richard Siddoway taught me a new way to look at the world, refine concepts, and communicate ideas. They came at the perfect time in my life and, for better or worse, helped shape the computer geek I am today.

Through those positive experiences and others, I had no reservations about diving in and experimenting with hardware and software on any platform, be it my beloved Apple II, my next passion the Commodore Amiga, and eventually the Macintosh.

As a university student, one department chair was impressed with my organizational, design and computer skills. I still feel proud that he often asked me, as a student in his class, to take the class to the Mac computer lab and teach them about desktop publishing – all by myself. It was an honor. I'm certain these experiences and skills contributed to my design and editing of books at Call-A.P.P.L.E. and elsewhere with things like my *Firefly* documentary film *Done The Impossible*.

Students asked me to tutor them and also repair their computers. Again, not something I ever had formal training for, but I suppose if one does something long enough, with enough passion and

self-education, one can develop many useful skills. After graduating, I pursued freelance technical consulting and design, along with many other completely different things like public speaking. Computers and all that they enable became my self-taught career.

I encourage you to embrace what you love – read, practice, talk with others, have fun, help others by volunteering, and ask. If there's one thing I've learned, perhaps only one thing :-), it never hurts to ask nicely. You may be amazed by unexpected opportunities that become possible if you are thoughtful and proactive. And it never hurts to be nice to people and help them. I guess that's two things! Try to be fearless and move forward with a positive goal. As someone once said, there are always possibilities and nothing is impossible.

Looking back with both lo-res and hi-res glasses, I'm so grateful for those early computing days and the friends and teachers who made it special. If only I could reboot my life with a PR#6 and experience it all again! Now where did I put that saved game disk?

Brian Wiser

April 2019

The Etch-a-Sketch

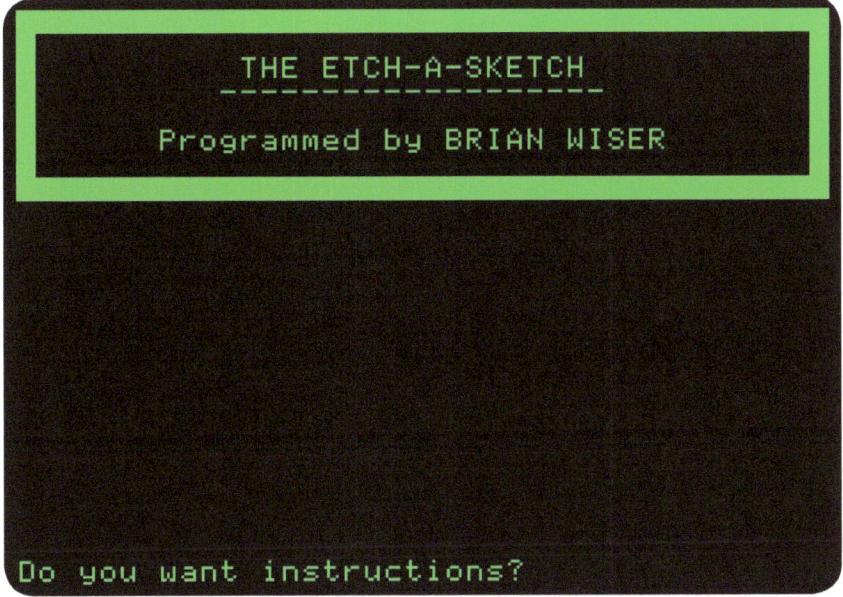

Being passionate about graphics and needing to submit a final project for Richard Siddoway's class, I created a tool that I dubbed *The Etch-a-Sketch*. I had fun imaging all the things I could do with it, like adding sound and joystick control to an otherwise simple drawing program. Over many months, its functions were refined and expanded.

Routines to HPLOT lines, draw shapes, and erase the screen were also added among other features. And I incorporated basic file utilities and several help pages. I had fun writing it and I wanted myself and any other potential users to have fun too!

When you first launch the program, it will ask if you want instructions and sound. The command keys are:

```
                U   I   O
                 \  |  /
    Drawing:    J - -|- - L
                 /  |  \
                M   K   .
```

1

Functions:

E – fast Erase mode
D – change Drawing location
F – Flash the pixel
P – hPlot a line
S – draw Shapes
H – Help screen
ESC – Toggle bottom graphics visibility
RETURN – Exit from option

Ctrl-L – Load picture
Ctrl-S – Save picture
Ctrl-I – change drawing Increment
Ctrl-E – Erase screen
Ctrl-R – Invert screen
Ctrl-J – use a Joystick
Ctrl-O – toggle Sound on-off
Ctrl-U – Utilities
Ctrl-Q – Quit

Change Drawing Color:

0 – Black 1
1 – Green
2 – Purple
3 – White 1
4 – Black 2
5 – Orange
6 – Blue
7 – White 2

Screen Dimensions:

Half Screen: 0 to 279 Horizontal, 0 to 159 Vertical
Full Screen: 0 to 279 Horizontal, 0 to 191 Vertical

```
10   REM ** THE ETCH-A-SKETCH **
20   REM *** BY BRIAN WISER ****
30   REM
40   REM
50   IF PEEK (104) < > 96 THEN POKE 24576,0: POKE
     104,96: PRINT CHR$ (4);"RUN THE ETCH-A-SKETCH"
60   ONERR GOTO 960
70   HC = 3:D$ = CHR$ (4): DIM MX(200),MY(200): PRINT
     D$;"NOMONICO": PRINT D$;"BLOAD INVERT": CALL
     16452: FOR A = 770 TO 792: READ B: POKE A,B: NEXT
     A: DATA  173,48,192,136,208,5,206,1,3,240,9,202,2
     08,245,174,0,3,76,2,3,96,0,0
75   REM
77   REM  *** TITLE PAGE ***
79   REM
80   HOME : INVERSE : PRINT "
     ";: PRINT " ";: HTAB 40: PRINT " ";: PRINT " ";:
     NORMAL : HTAB 12: PRINT "THE ETCH-A-SKETCH";: HTAB
     40: INVERSE : PRINT " ";:PRINT " ";: NORMAL
85   HTAB 11: PRINT "-------------------";: HTAB 40:
     INVERSE
90   PRINT " ";: PRINT " ";: HTAB 40: PRINT " ";:
     PRINT " ";: NORMAL : HTAB 8: PRINT "Programmed
     by BRIAN WISER";: HTAB 40: INVERSE : PRINT "
     ";: PRINT " ";: HTAB 40: PRINT " ";: PRINT "
     ": NORMAL
100  VTAB 24: PRINT "Do you want instructions? ";:GET
     A$
120  IF A$ = "Y" OR A$ = "y" THEN 150
130  IF A$ = "N" OR A$ = "n" OR A$ = CHR$ (13) THEN 260
140  GOTO 110
145  REM
147  REM  *** HELP SCREENS ***
149  REM
150  HOME : HTAB 29: PRINT "U I O": HTAB 29: PRINT "
     \|/ ": PRINT "The keys used to draw are:  ";:
     PRINT "J-|-L": HTAB 29: PRINT " /|\ ": HTAB 29:
     PRINT "M K ."
155  VTAB 7: PRINT "E - fast Erase mode": PRINT :
     PRINT "D - change Drawing location": PRINT :
     PRINT "F - Flash the pixel"
```

3

```
160  PRINT : PRINT "P - hPlot a line": PRINT : PRINT
     "S - draw Shapes": PRINT : PRINT "H - Help
     screen"
165  PRINT : PRINT "ESC - Toggle bottom graphics
     visibility": PRINT : PRINT "RETURN - Exit from
     option": VTAB 24: PRINT "Press any key to
     continue...";: GET A$: HOME : HTAB 14
170  PRINT "CONTROL KEYS": HTAB 13: PRINT "-----------
     ---": VTAB 5: INVERSE : PRINT "CTRL-L";: NORMAL :
     PRINT " - Load picture": INVERSE
175  PRINT : PRINT "CTRL-S";: NORMAL : PRINT " - Save
     picture": INVERSE : PRINT : PRINT "CTRL-I";:
     NORMAL : PRINT " - change drawing Increment":
     INVERSE
180  PRINT : PRINT "CTRL-E";: NORMAL : PRINT " - Erase
     screen": INVERSE : PRINT : PRINT "CTRL-R";:
     NORMAL : PRINT " - Invert screen": INVERSE :
     PRINT : PRINT "CTRL-J";: NORMAL : PRINT " - use a
     Joystick"
190  INVERSE : PRINT : PRINT "CTRL-O";: NORMAL : PRINT
     " - toggle Sound on-off": INVERSE : PRINT : PRINT
     "CTRL-U";: NORMAL : PRINT " - Utilities"
200  INVERSE : PRINT : PRINT "CTRL-Q";: NORMAL : PRINT
     " - Quit": VTAB 24: PRINT "Press any key to
     continue...";: GET A$
205  HOME : HTAB 17: PRINT "COLORS": HTAB 16: PRINT
     "--------": VTAB 4: PRINT "To change the drawing
     color, press the  color number you want:"
210  VTAB 8: HTAB 17: PRINT "0 - Black 1": VTAB 10:
     HTAB 17: PRINT "1 - Green": VTAB 12: HTAB 17:
     PRINT "2 - Purple": VTAB 14: HTAB 17: PRINT "3 -
     White 1": VTAB 16: HTAB 17: PRINT "4 - Black 2"
215  VTAB 18: HTAB 17: PRINT "5 - Orange": VTAB 20:
     HTAB 17: PRINT "6 - Blue": VTAB 22: HTAB 17:
     PRINT "7 - White 2": VTAB 24: PRINT "Press any
     key to continue...";: GET A$: HOME
220  HTAB 8: PRINT "DIMENSIONS OF THE SCREEN": HTAB 7:
     PRINT "-------------------------": VTAB 5: HTAB
     5: PRINT "HALF SCREEN": HTAB 4: PRINT "---------
     ----"
225  PRINT : HTAB 6: PRINT "0----279": HTAB 6: PRINT
```

```
      "'";: INVERSE : PRINT "          ": NORMAL : HTAB 6:
      PRINT "1";: INVERSE
230   PRINT "          ": NORMAL : HTAB 6: PRINT "5";:
      INVERSE : PRINT "          ": NORMAL : HTAB 6: PRINT
      "9";: INVERSE : PRINT "          ": NORMAL : VTAB 5:
      HTAB 25: PRINT "FULL SCREEN": HTAB 24: PRINT "---
      ----------"
235   PRINT : HTAB 26: PRINT "0----279": HTAB 26: PRINT
      "'";: INVERSE : PRINT "          ": NORMAL
240   HTAB 26: PRINT "'";: INVERSE : PRINT "          ":
      NORMAL : HTAB 26: PRINT "1";: INVERSE : PRINT "
      ": NORMAL : HTAB 26: PRINT "9";: INVERSE : PRINT
      "          ": NORMAL : HTAB 26: PRINT "1";
245   INVERSE : PRINT "          ": NORMAL : VTAB 24:
      PRINT "Press any key to continue...";: GET A$
250   IF V = 1 THEN POKE - 16304,0: HOME : GOTO 290
255   REM
257   REM    *** SOUND CHOICE ***
259   REM
260   H = 1: HOME: VTAB 1: PRINT "Do you want sound?
      ";: GET A$: IF A$ < > "Y" AND A$ < > "y" THEN Z
      = 0: GOTO 280
270   Z = 1
280   X = 140:Y = 80:A1 = X:B1 = Y: HGR: HCOLOR= 3:
      HPLOT X,Y: GOSUB 720
285   REM
287   REM   *** MAIN PROGRAM ***
289   REM
290   VTAB 21: HTAB 1: PRINT "X=";X;"  ": PRINT
      "Y=";Y;"  ";: HTAB 15: PRINT "Type 'H' for Help":
      PRINT "C=";HC: PRINT "I=";H;: VTAB 9: GET A$:F = 0
300   IF A$ = "F" OR A$ = "f" THEN HPLOT X,Y: HCOLOR=
      0: HPLOT X,Y: HCOLOR= 3
310   IF A$ = "F" OR A$ = "f" AND F = 45 THEN HCOLOR=
      HC: GOTO 340
320   IF A$ = "F" OR A$ = "f" THEN F = F + 1: GOTO 300
330   IF A$ = "I" OR A$ = "i" THEN Y = Y - H
340   IF A$ = "K" OR A$ = "k" THEN Y = Y + H
350   IF A$ = "J" OR A$ = "j" THEN X = X - H
360   IF A$ = "L" OR A$ = "l" THEN X = X + H
370   IF A$ = "U" OR A$ = "u" THEN Y = Y - H:X = X - H
```

5

```
380  IF A$ = "O" OR A$ = "o" THEN Y = Y - H:X = X + H
390  IF A$ = "M" OR A$ = "m" THEN Y = Y + H:X = X - H
400  IF A$ = "." THEN Y = Y + H:X = X + H
410  IF A$ = "E" OR A$ = "e" THEN  GOSUB 1090
420  IF A$ = "D" OR A$ = "d" THEN L = 1: GOSUB 750
430  IF A$ = "P" OR A$ = "p" THEN  HOME : VTAB 24:
     INPUT "Enter the first X and Y values: ";X2,Y2:
     HOME : VTAB 24: INPUT "Enter the last X and Y
     values: ";X3,Y3: HPLOT X2,Y2 TO X3,Y3: HOME :
     GOSUB 1330: GOTO 290
440  IF A$ = "S" OR A$ = "s" THEN 1750
450  IF A$ = "H" OR A$ = "h" THEN  TEXT :V = 1: GOTO 150
455  REM
457  REM  *** ESC-TOGGLE GRAPHICS ***
459  REM
460  IF A$ =  CHR$ (27) AND FS = 0 THEN FS = 1: POKE -
     16302,0: GOTO 290
470  IF A$ =  CHR$ (27) AND FS = 1 THEN FS = 0: POKE -
     16301,0: GOTO 290
475  REM
477  REM  *** LOAD PICTURE ***
479  REM
480  IF A$ =  CHR$ (12) THEN  HOME : VTAB 24: INPUT
     "Picture to Load: ";L$: HOME : IF L$ = "" THEN 290
490  IF A$ =  CHR$ (12) THEN  VTAB 23: HTAB 11: PRINT
     "LOADING PICTURE...": PRINT D$;"BLOAD ";L$:X =
     140:Y = 80:A1 = X:B1 = Y: HCOLOR= 3:HC = 3:H = 1:
     HOME
500  IF A$ = CHR$ (19) THEN  GOTO 1680
505  REM
507  REM  *** DRAWING INCREMENT ***
509  REM
510  IF A$ = CHR$ (9) THEN  HOME : VTAB 24: INPUT
     "Increment: ";H: HOME : IF H = 0 THEN H = 1
520  IF H < 0 OR H > 279 THEN H = 1
530  IF A$ = CHR$ (5) THEN  GOSUB 880
535  REM
537  REM  *** INVERSE SCREEN ***
539  REM
540  IF A$ = CHR$ (18) THEN  CALL 16384
545  REM
```

```
547    REM  *** JOYSTICK GOTO ***
549    REM
550    IF A$ = CHR$ (10) THEN  GOSUB 1350
555    REM
557    REM  *** SOUND TOGGLE ***
559    REM
560    IF A$ = CHR$ (15) AND Z = 0 THEN Z = 1:A$ = ""
570    IF A$ = CHR$ (15) AND Z = 1 THEN Z = 0
575    REM
577    REM  *** UTILITIES GOTO ***
579    REM
580    IF A$ = CHR$ (21) THEN 1530
585    REM
587    REM  *** QUIT ***
589    REM
590    IF A$ = CHR$ (17) THEN  HOME : VTAB 24: PRINT
       "Are you sure you want to quit? ";: GET V$: HOME
       : IF V$ = "Y" OR V$ = "y" THEN  TEXT : HOME : END
591    REM
593    REM  *** COLOR CHANGE ***
595    REM
596    IF A$ = "0" THEN  HCOLOR= 0:HC = 0
600    IF A$ = "1" THEN  HCOLOR= 1:HC = 1
610    IF A$ = "2" THEN  HCOLOR= 2:HC = 2
620    IF A$ = "3" THEN  HCOLOR= 3:HC = 3
630    IF A$ = "4" THEN  HCOLOR= 4:HC = 4
640    IF A$ = "5" THEN  HCOLOR= 5:HC = 5
650    IF A$ = "6" THEN  HCOLOR= 6:HC = 6
655    IF A$ = "7" THEN  HCOLOR= 7:HC = 7
660    X1 = X:Y1 = Y
670    IF X > 279 OR X < 0 THEN X = A1
680    IF Y > 191 OR Y < 0 THEN Y = B1
690    IF H = 1 THEN  HPLOT X,Y: GOTO 710
700    HPLOT A1,B1 TO X,Y
710    A1 = X:B1 = Y
715    REM
717    REM  *** SOUND ***
719    REM
720    IF Z = 1 THEN Z% = (X + Y) / 2: POKE 768,Z%: POKE
       769,5: CALL 770
730    L = 0
```

```
740   GOTO 290
745   REM
747   REM   *** DRAWING LOCATION ***
749   REM
750   HOME : VTAB 24: PRINT "Do you want to erase the
      last point? ";: GET EP$: IF EP$ =  CHR$ (13) THEN
      HOME : GOTO 290
755   IF C% = 0 THEN Q% = 0
760   IF C% = 1 THEN Q% = 2
770   IF C% = 2 THEN Q% = 1
780   IF C% = 3 THEN Q% = 3
790   IF C% = 4 THEN Q% = 4
800   IF C% = 5 THEN Q% = 6
810   IF C% = 6 THEN Q% = 5
815   IF C% = 7 THEN Q% = 7
820   IF EP$ = "Y" THEN  HCOLOR= Q%: HPLOT X,Y: HCOLOR= HC
830   HOME : VTAB 23: PRINT "Starting Point:
      X=";X: VTAB 23: INVERSE : HTAB 27: PRINT
      "RETURN=CENTER";: NORMAL : VTAB 23: HTAB 19:
      INPUT "";X$:X = VAL (X$): IF X < 0 OR X > 279
      THEN 830
840   IF X$ = "" THEN X = 140:Y = 80:A1 = X:B1 = Y:
      HOME : GOTO 870
850   VTAB 24: HTAB 17: PRINT "Y=";Y;: HTAB 19: INPUT
      "";Y$:Y =  VAL (Y$): IF Y < 0 OR Y > 191 THEN 830
860   A1 = X:B1 = Y: HOME
870   IF L = 1 THEN  RETURN
880   X = 140:Y = 80:A1 = X:B1 = Y: HOME : VTAB 24:
      INPUT "Erase to which Background Color 0-7? ";C$:
      IF C$ = "" OR C$ = "4" THEN  HGR : HCOLOR= 3:C% =
      4:HC = 3:H = 1: HOME : RETURN
890   C% =  VAL (C$)
900   IF C% < 0 OR C% > 7 THEN 880
910   IF C% = 1 THEN HC = 1
920   IF C% = 2 THEN HC = 3
930   IF C% = 3 OR C% = 5 OR C% = 7 THEN HC = 4
940   IF C% = 6 THEN HC = 6
950   HOME : HGR : HCOLOR= C%: HPLOT 9,9: CALL 62454:
      HCOLOR= HC:H = 1: RETURN
```

```
955   REM
957   REM  *** UTILITIES ERRORS ***
959   REM
960   IF PEEK (222) = 4 THEN HOME: VTAB 23: HTAB 10:
      PRINT "---WRITE PROTECTED---": FOR P = 1 TO 1500:
      NEXT P
970   IF PEEK (222) = 6 THEN HOME: VTAB 23: HTAB 10:
      PRINT "---FILE NOT FOUND---": FOR P = 1 TO 1500:
      NEXT P
980   IF PEEK (222) = 8 THEN HOME: VTAB 23: HTAB 13:
      PRINT "---I/O ERROR---": FOR P = 1 TO 1500: NEXT P
990   IF PEEK (222) = 9 THEN HOME: VTAB 23: HTAB 13:
      PRINT "---DISK FULL---": FOR P = 1 TO 1500:
      NEXT P: HOME: VTAB 23: HTAB 12: PRINT "DELETING
      FILE...";: PRINT : PRINT D$;"DELETE ";S$
1000  IF  PEEK (222) = 10 THEN  HOME : VTAB 23: HTAB
      12: PRINT "---FILE LOCKED---": FOR P = 1 TO
      1500: NEXT P: HOME : VTAB 24: PRINT "Do you want
      to resave the picture? ";: GET UF$
1005  IF UF$ = "Y" THEN  HOME : VTAB 23: HTAB 12:
      PRINT "UNLOCKING FILE...";: PRINT : PRINT
      D$;"UNLOCK ";S$
1010  IF  PEEK (222) = 10 AND UF$ = "Y" THEN  HOME :
      VTAB 23: HTAB 12: PRINT "RESAVING PICTURE...";:
      PRINT : PRINT D$;"BSAVE ";S$;",A$2000,L$2000"
1020  IF  PEEK (222) = 11 THEN  HOME : GOTO 290
1030  IF  PEEK (222) = 13 THEN  HOME : VTAB 23: HTAB 8:
      PRINT "---FILE TYPE MISMATCH---": FOR P = 1 TO
      1500: NEXT P
1040  IF  PEEK (222) = 16 THEN  HOME : GOTO 290
1050  IF  PEEK (222) = 69 THEN  HOME : GOTO 290
1060  IF  PEEK (222) = 254 AND H = 0 THEN H = 1
1070  IF  PEEK (222) = 255 THEN  POKE  - 16304,0
1080  HOME : GOTO 290
1085  REM
1087  REM  *** ERASE MODE ***
1089  REM
1090  HOME : VTAB 24: PRINT "What color 0-7 to Fast
      Erase with? ";: GET C%: HOME
```

```
1100  K =  PEEK ( - 16384)
1110  A1 = X:B1 = Y:K = K - 128
1120  VTAB 21: HTAB 1: PRINT "X=";X;"   ": PRINT
      "Y=";Y;"   ";: HTAB 14: PRINT "Type 'R' to
      Return": PRINT "C=";C%: PRINT "I=";H;
1130  IF K = 73 OR K = 105 THEN Y = Y - H
1140  IF K = 75 OR K = 107 THEN Y = Y + H
1150  IF K = 74 OR K = 106 THEN X = X - H
1160  IF K = 76 OR K = 108 THEN X = X + H
1170  IF K = 85 OR K = 117 THEN Y = Y - H:X = X - H
1180  IF K = 79 OR K = 111 THEN Y = Y - H:X = X + H
1190  IF K = 77 OR K = 109 THEN Y = Y + H:X = X - H
1200  IF K = 46 THEN Y = Y + H:X = X + H
1210  IF K = 82 OR K = 114 THEN  HOME : HCOLOR= HC:
      GOTO 290
1220  IF X > 279 OR X < 0 THEN X = A1
1230  IF Y > 191 OR Y < 0 THEN Y = B1
1240  HCOLOR= HC: HPLOT X,Y: HCOLOR= C%: IF H > 1 THEN
      HPLOT A1,B1 TO X,Y
1250  HPLOT A1,B1
1260  IF Z = 1 THEN Z% = (X + Y) / 2: POKE 768,Z%:
      POKE 769,3: CALL 770
1270  GOTO 1100
1275  REM
1277  REM  *** SHAPES - CIRCLES ***
1279  REM
1280  POKE  - 16304,0: HOME : VTAB 24: INPUT "Enter
      X and Y Coordinates: ";XC,YC: HOME : VTAB 24:
      INPUT "Enter X and Y Radius: ";XX,YY: HOME :
      VTAB 24: INPUT "Step Size: ";SV
1285  HOME: VTAB 24: PRINT "Do you want it to be
      filled? ";: GET CC$: HOME : VTAB 23: HTAB 12
1290  PRINT "DRAWING CIRCLE...": HPLOT XC + XX,YC: FOR
      VS = 1 TO 102 STEP (SV * .2):XR =  INT ( COS (VS
      / 16) * XX) + XC:YR =  INT ( SIN (VS / 16) * YY)
      + YC: IF YR > 191 OR YR < 0 OR XR > 279 OR XR <
      0 THEN 1320
1300  HPLOT  TO XR,YR: IF CC$ = "Y" THEN  HPLOT XC,YC
      TO XR,YR
1310  IF Z = 1 THEN Z% = (XR + YR) / 2: POKE 768,Z%:
      POKE 769,3: CALL 770
```

```
1320  NEXT : HOME : GOTO 290
1325  REM
1327  REM   *** HPLOT SUBROUTINE ***
1329  REM
1330  IF Z = 1 THEN Z% = (X2 + Y2 + Y3 + X3) / 4: POKE
      768,Z%: POKE 769,5: CALL 770
1340  RETURN
1345  REM
1347  REM   *** JOYSTICK ***
1349  REM
1350  HOME : HCOLOR= HC
1360  YY =  PDL (1):XX =  PDL (0)
1370  IF XX > 225 AND YY < 10 THEN Y = Y - H:X = X +
      H: GOTO 1420
1380  IF XX > 245 THEN X = X + H
1390  IF XX < 10 THEN X = X - H
1400  IF YY > 245 THEN Y = Y + H
1410  IF YY < 10 THEN Y = Y - H
1420  IF X > 279 THEN X = 279
1430  IF X < 0 THEN X = 0
1440  IF Y > 191 THEN Y = 191
1450  IF Y < 0 THEN Y = 0
1460  IF H = 1 THEN  HPLOT X,Y
1470  HPLOT  TO X,Y
1480  KEY =  PEEK ( - 16384): POKE  - 16368,0
1490  IF KEY > 127 THEN  HOME :A1 = X:B1 = Y: RETURN
1500  B = B + 1
1510  IF Z = 1 THEN Z% = (X + Y) / 2: POKE 768,Z%:
      POKE 769,25: CALL 770
1520  VTAB 21: HTAB 1: PRINT "X=";X;"  ": PRINT
      "Y=";Y;"  ";: HTAB 13: PRINT "Press any key to
      return": PRINT "C=";HC: PRINT "I=";H;: GOTO 1360
1525  REM
1527  REM   *** UTILITIES ***
1529  REM
1530  POKE 216,0: ONERR  GOTO 1640
1540  TEXT : HOME : HTAB 16: PRINT "UTILITIES": HTAB
      15: PRINT "-----------": VTAB 4: PRINT "1 -
      Catalog disk": PRINT "2 - Lock file": PRINT "3
      - Unlock file": PRINT "4 - Delete file": PRINT
      "5 - Rename file": PRINT "6 - Exit"
```

```
1545   PRINT : PRINT "Option: ";: GET A
1550   IF A < 1 OR A > 6 THEN 1540
1560   ON A GOTO 1570,1580,1590,1600,1610,1620
1570   POKE 44452,24: POKE 44605,23: HOME : PRINT :
       PRINT D$;"CATALOG": PRINT : PRINT "Press any key
       to return to Menu...";: GET A$: GOTO 1540
1580   HOME : VTAB 12: INPUT "File to Lock: ";LK$: HOME
       : VTAB 12: HTAB 13: PRINT "LOCKING FILE...":
       PRINT : PRINT D$;"LOCK ";LK$: GOTO 1540
1590   HOME : VTAB 12: INPUT "File to Unlock: ";UK$:
       HOME : VTAB 12: HTAB 12: PRINT "UNLOCKING
       FILE...": PRINT : PRINT D$;"UNLOCK ";UK$: GOTO 1540
1600   HOME : VTAB 12: INPUT "File to Delete: ";DL$:
       HOME : VTAB 12: HTAB 12: PRINT "DELETING
       FILE...": PRINT : PRINT D$;"DELETE ";DL$: GOTO 1540
1610   HOME : VTAB 12: INPUT "File to Rename: ";RN$:
       HOME : VTAB 12: INPUT "New Name: ";NM$: HOME
       : VTAB 12: HTAB 12: PRINT "RENAMING FILE...":
       PRINT : PRINT D$;"RENAME ";RN$;",";NM$: GOTO 1540
1620   POKE 216,0: ONERR  GOTO 960
1630   POKE  - 16304,0: HOME : GOTO 290
1640   IF  PEEK (222) = 6 THEN  HOME : VTAB 12: HTAB
       10: PRINT "---FILE NOT FOUND---": FOR P = 1 TO
       1500: NEXT P
1650   IF  PEEK (222) = 10 THEN  HOME : VTAB 12: HTAB
       12: PRINT "---FILE LOCKED---": FOR P = 1 TO
       1500: NEXT P
1660   IF  PEEK (222) = 4 THEN  HOME : VTAB 12: HTAB
       10: PRINT "---WRITE PROTECTED---": FOR P = 1 TO
       1500: NEXT P
1670   GOTO 1540
1675   REM
1677   REM  *** SAVE PICTURE ***
1679   REM
1680   HOME : VTAB 24: INPUT "Picture to Save: ";S$:
       HOME : IF S$ = "" THEN 290
1690   POKE 216,0: ONERR  GOTO 1710
1700   VTAB 23: HTAB 12: PRINT "SAVING PICTURE...";:
       PRINT: PRINT D$;"VERIFY ";S$: HOME: VTAB 23:
       HTAB 8: PRINT "---FILE ALREADY EXISTS---": FOR P
       = 1 TO 1500: NEXT P
```

```
1705  HOME : VTAB 24: PRINT "Do you want to replace
      it? ";: GET RC$: IF RC$ <  > "Y" THEN  HOME :
      GOTO 1730
1710  POKE 216,0: ONERR  GOTO 960
1720  HOME : VTAB 23: HTAB 12: PRINT "SAVING
      PICTURE...";: PRINT : PRINT D$;"BSAVE ";S$;",
      A$2000,L$2000": HOME : GOTO 290
1730  POKE 216,0: ONERR  GOTO 960
1740  GOTO 290
1745  REM
1747  REM   *** DRAW SHAPES ***
1749  REM
1750  POKE 216,0: ONERR  GOTO 1760
1760  TEXT : HOME : HTAB 17: PRINT "SHAPES": HTAB 16:
      PRINT "--------": VTAB 4: PRINT "1 - Circles":
      PRINT "2 - Spirals #1": PRINT "3 - Spirals #2"
1765  PRINT "4 - Polygons": PRINT "5 - Inscribed
      Polygons": PRINT "6 - Return to Editor": PRINT :
      PRINT "Option: ";: GET SH
1770  IF SH < 1 OR SH > 6 THEN 1760
1780  POKE 216,0: ONERR  GOTO 960
1790  ON SH GOTO 1280,1800,1860,1900,1950,2020
1795  REM
1797  REM   *** SHAPES - SPIRALS #1 ***
1799  REM
1800  POKE  - 16304,0: HOME : VTAB 24: INPUT "Enter X
      and Y Coordinates: ";G1,G2
1810  HOME : VTAB 24: INPUT "Angle: ";AN:NA = AN: IF
      AN = 0 THEN 1810
1820  HOME : VTAB 23: HTAB 12: PRINT "DRAWING
      SPIRAL..."
1830  G = .0174 * AN:GL = AN / NA:G3 = G1 + GL *  COS
      (G):G4 = G2 - GL *  SIN (G): HPLOT G1,G2 TO G3,G4
1840  IF Z = 1 THEN Z% = (G1 + G2 + G3 + G4) / 4: POKE
      768,Z%: POKE 769,3: CALL 770
1850  AN = AN + NA:G1 = G3:G2 = G4: GOTO 1830
1855  REM
1857  REM   *** SHAPES - SPIRALS #2 ***
1859  REM
```

```
1860  POKE  - 16304,0: HOME : VTAB 24: INPUT "Enter
      X and Y Coordinates: ";I1,I2: HOME : VTAB 24:
      INPUT "Difference in Degrees: ";ID:ID = ID
      / 57.29578: HOME : VTAB 23: HTAB 12: PRINT
      "DRAWING SPIRAL...": HPLOT I1,I2
1870  FOR IR = 0 TO 200 STEP ID:IX = I1 + IR *  COS
      (IR):IY = I2 + 0.7 * (IR *  SIN (IR)): HPLOT TO IX,IY
1880  IF Z = 1 THEN Z% = (IX + IY) / 2: POKE 768,Z%:
      POKE 769,4: CALL 770
1890  NEXT
1895  REM
1897  REM  *** SHAPES - POLYGONS ***
1899  REM
1900  POKE  - 16304,0: HOME : VTAB 24: INPUT "Enter
      X and Y Coordinates: ";CX,CY: HOME : VTAB 24:
      INPUT "Number of Sides: ";S: HOME : VTAB 24:
      INPUT "Radius: ";RD: HOME : IF CX - RD < 0 OR CX
      + RD > 279 THEN 1900
1910  IF CY - RD < 0 OR CY + RD > 191 THEN 1900
1920  IF CX > 279 OR CY > 191 OR CX < 0 OR CY < 0 THEN
      1900
1930  HOME : VTAB 23: HTAB 11: PRINT "DRAWING
      POLYGON...":A =  ATN (1) * 8 / S: HPLOT CX,CY +
      RD: FOR I = A TO  ATN (1) * 8 STEP A: HPLOT  TO
      CX +  SIN (I) * RD,CY +  COS (I) * RD
1935  IF Z = 1 THEN Z% = (CX + CY + RD +  SIN (I) +
      COS (I)) / 5: POKE 768,Z%: POKE 769,3: CALL 770
1940  NEXT I: HPLOT  TO CX,CY + RD: HOME : GOTO 290
1945  REM
1947  REM  *** INSCRIBED POLYGONS ***
1949  REM
1950  POKE  - 16304,0: HOME : VTAB 24: INPUT "Enter X
      and Y Coordinates: ";M1,M2
1960  HOME : VTAB 24: INPUT "Size: ";MR: IF MR < 1 OR
      MR > 88 THEN 1960
1970  HOME : VTAB 24: INPUT "Number of Sides: ";MN: IF
      MN < 3 OR MN > 200 THEN 1970
1980  HOME : VTAB 23: HTAB 10: PRINT "CALCULATING
      POINTS...": GOSUB 2010: HOME : VTAB 23: HTAB 11:
      PRINT "DRAWING POLYGON...": FOR MJ = 1 TO MN -
```

14

```
      1: FOR MK = MJ + 1 TO MN: HPLOT M1 + MX(MJ),M2 +
         MY(MJ) TO M1 + MX(MK),M2 + MY(MK)
1990     IF Z = 1 THEN Z% = (M1 + MX(MJ) + M2 + MY(MJ)
         + M1 + MX(MK) + M2 + MY(MK)) / 8: POKE 768,Z%:
         POKE 769,4: CALL 770
2000     NEXT MK: NEXT MJ: HOME : GOTO 290
2010     FOR MI = 1 TO MN:MD = MI * 360 / MN:MA = MD *
         3.1415926 / 180:MX(MI) = MR *  COS (MA):MY(MI)
         = MR *  SIN (MA):MY(MI) =  - MY(MI) / 1.1: NEXT
         MI: RETURN
2020     POKE  - 16304,0: HOME : GOTO 290
```

"Pyramid" by Brian Wiser (drawn with *The Etch-a-Sketch*)

The Apple

This was the result of a lesson on low-resolution graphics. After the program runs and you're finished gazing, type "TEXT" to switch to the text screen. Clearly, I was in love with Apple and the computers they produced, courtesy of Woz. Did I mention that I took a photo of Steve Wozniak from an Applied Engineering ad and made a button? Try not to laugh at me too much when I tell you that I attached it to the front of my Apple IIGS :-)

```
1  REM  ***** THE APPLE ******
2  REM  *** BY BRIAN WISER ***
3  REM
4  REM
10  TEXT : HOME : GR : FOR A = 1 TO 85
20  READ B,C: COLOR= 1: PLOT B,C: NEXT A
```

```
30  DATA  1,4,1,5,1,6,1,7,2,3,2,5,3,4,3,5,3,6,3,7,5,
    3,5,4,5,5,5,6,5,7,6,3,6,5,7,3,7,4,7,5,9,3,9,4,9,
    5,9,6,9,7,10,3,10,5,11,3,11,4,11,5,13,3,13,4,13,
    5,13,6,13,7,14,7,16,3,16,4,16,5,16,6,16,7,17,3,
    17,5,17,7
40  DATA  21,3,21,7,22,3,22,4,22,5,22,6,22,7,23,3,23,
    7,25,3,25,4,25,5,25,7,26,3,26,5,26,6,26,7,30,4,
    30,6,31,3,31,4,31,5,31,6,31,7,32,4,32,6,33,3,33,
    4,33,5,33,6,33,7,34,4,34,6,36,3,36,7,37,3,37,4,
    37,5,37,6,37,7,38,7
50  COLOR= 12: VLIN 13,16 AT 20: VLIN 12,15 AT 21:
    VLIN 11,14 AT 22: FOR A = 1 TO 25: READ D,E,F,G:
    COLOR= G: HLIN D,E AT F: NEXT A
60  DATA  17,17,16,12,23,24,16,12,16,18,17,12,22,25,
    17,12,15,26,18,12,14,26,19,12,14,27,20,12,13,26,
    21,13,13,25,22,13,13,25,23,13,13,24,24,9,13,24,
    25,9,13,24,26,9,13,25,27,1,13,25,28,1,13,26,29,1,
    14,27,30,3,14,27,31,3,15,27,32,3
70  DATA  15,26,33,6,15,26,34,6,16,19,35,6,21,25,35,6,
    17,18,36,6,22,25,36,6
```

Motherboard Simulation

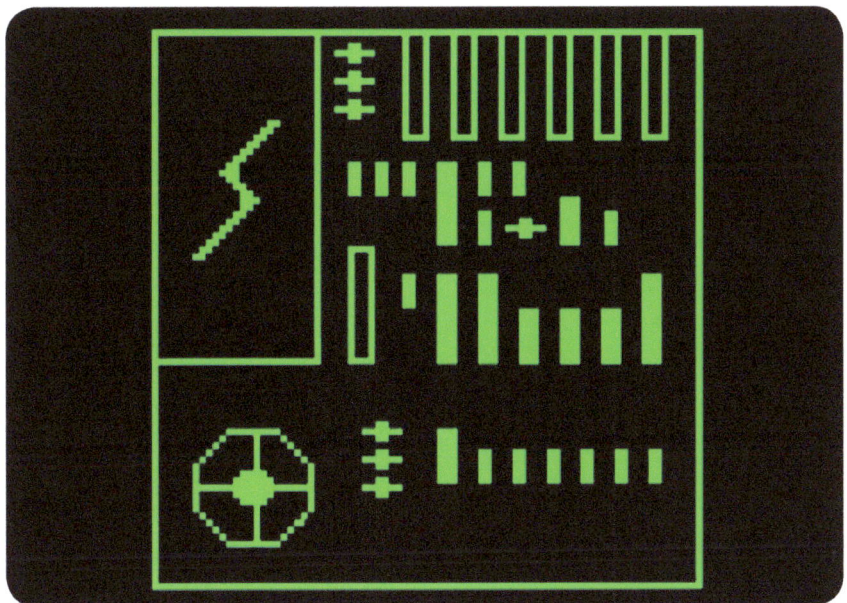

My machine language teacher assigned this concept for my final exam. I suspect it was inspired by RPG games where one moved around a picture in memory. Here, I've created a simple picture of an Apple IIe motherboard that's partially visible through a window, and defined keys for movement:

```
              I
      Move: J + L        Quit: Q
              K
```

This was written in *Big Mac* and the source code file is "MOTHERBOARD SIMULATION.S". In the assembled listing, the version on the left shows the addresses of each assembled instruction and the hexadecimal values those instructions were converted to. The line numbers are in the middle, and more-readable source is on the right. The first line dictates that the machine language routine will start at address $6D00 in memory. That's where the assembler will start putting the instructions.

:ASM

```
                      1              ORG   $6D00
6D00:  20 58 FC       2              JSR   $FC58
6D03:  AE 6D 6D       3       TEXT2  LDX   INFO2
6D06:  8E 8E 07       4       LD2    STX   $78E
6D09:  EE 04 6D       5              INC   TEXT2+1
6D0C:  EE 07 6D       6              INC   LD2+1
6D0F:  AC 07 6D       7              LDY   LD2+1
6D12:  C0 9A          8              CPY   #$9A
6D14:  D0 ED          9              BNE   TEXT2
6D16:  AE 79 6D      10       TEXT3  LDX   INFO3
6D19:  8E B1 04      11       LD3    STX   $4B1
6D1C:  EE 17 6D      12              INC   TEXT3+1
6D1F:  EE 1A 6D      13              INC   LD3+1
6D22:  AC 1A 6D      14              LDY   LD3+1
6D25:  C0 C6         15              CPY   #$C6
6D27:  D0 ED         16              BNE   TEXT3
6D29:  AE 8E 6D      17       TEXT4  LDX   INFO4
6D2C:  8E B3 05      18       LD4    STX   $5B3
6D2F:  EE 2A 6D      19              INC   TEXT4+1
6D32:  EE 2D 6D      20              INC   LD4+1
6D35:  AC 2D 6D      21              LDY   LD4+1
6D38:  C0 C4         22              CPY   #$C4
6D3A:  D0 ED         23              BNE   TEXT4
6D3C:  AE 9F 6D      24       TEXT5  LDX   INFO5
6D3F:  8E AA 06      25       LD5    STX   $6AA
6D42:  EE 3D 6D      26              INC   TEXT5+1
6D45:  EE 40 6D      27              INC   LD5+1
6D48:  AC 40 6D      28              LDY   LD5+1
6D4B:  C0 CE          9              CPY   #$CE
6D4D:  D0 ED         30              BNE   TEXT5
6D4F:  AE C3 6D      31       TEXT6  LDX   INFO6
6D52:  8E D0 07      32       LD6    STX   $7D0
6D55:  EE 50 6D      33              INC   TEXT6+1
6D58:  EE 53 6D      34              INC   LD6+1
6D5B:  AC 53 6D      35              LDY   LD6+1
6D5E:  C0 EC         36              CPY   #$EC
6D60:  D0 ED         37              BNE   TEXT6
6D62:  8D 10 C0      38              STA   $C010
6D65:  AD 00 C0      39       BLAH   LDA   $C000
6D68:  10 FB         40              BPL   BLAH
```

```
6D6A: 4C DF 6D     41                        JMP   RGB
6D6D: C1 A0 D3
6D70: E9 ED F5
6D73: EC E1 F4
6D76: E9 EF EE     42    INFO2     ASC   "A Simulation"
6D79: A0 CF E6
6D7C: A0 E1 A0
6D7F: C9 C9 E5
6D82: A0 CD EF
6D85: F4 E8 E5
6D88: F2 E2 EF
6D8B: E1 F2 E4     43    INFO3     ASC "Of a IIe Motherboard"
6D8E: A0 A0 E2
6D91: F9 A0 C2
6D94: F2 E9 E1
6D97: EE A0 D7
6D9A: E9 F3 E5
6D9D: F2 A0        44    INFO4     ASC   "by Brian Wiser"
6D9F: A0 A0 A0
6DA2: A0 A0 A0
6DA5: A0 A0 A0
6DA8: A0 A0 A0
6DAB: A0 A0 A0
6DAE: A0 A0 A0
6DB1: A0 A0 A0
6DB4: A0 A0 A0
6DB7: A0 A0 A0
6DBA: A0 A0 A0
6DBD: A0 A0 A0
6DC0: A0 A0 A0     45    INFO5     ASC   "                    "
6DC3: D0 F2 E5
6DC6: F3 F3 A0
6DC9: C1 EE F9
6DCC: A0 CB E5
6DCF: F9 A0 F4
6DD2: EF A0 C3
6DD5: EF EE F4
6DD8: E9 EE F5
6DDB: E5 AE AE
6DDE: AE           46    INFO6     ASC "Press Any Key to
                                         Continue..."
```

```
6DDF: A9 64        47   RGB        LDA  #$64
6DE1: 8D 18 6E     48              STA  DATA+2
6DE4: 8D 20 03     49              STA  $320
6DE7: A9 18        50              LDA  #$18
6DE9: 8D 17 6E     51              STA  DATA+1
6DEC: 8D 21 03     52              STA  $321
6DEF: A2 03        53              LDX  #$03
6DF1: 8E 10 03     54              STX  $310
6DF4: A2 04        55              LDX  #$04
6DF6: 8E 11 03     56              STX  $311
6DF9: 20 E2 F3     57              JSR  $F3E2
6DFC: 20 F2 F3     58              JSR  $F3F2
6DFF: A2 00        59   CHECK      LDX  #$00
6E01: 8E 00 03     60              STX  $300
6E04: 8E 02 03     61              STX  $302
6E07: A9 20        62              LDA  #$20
6E09: 8D 1B 6E     63              STA  LOCATION+2
6E0C: A9 28        64              LDA  #$28
6E0E: 8D 1A 6E     65              STA  LOCATION+1
6E11: 20 58 FC     66              JSR  $FC58
6E14: A0 12        67              LDY  #$12
6E16: AD 18 64     68   DATA       LDA  $6418
6E19: 99 28 20     69   LOCATION   STA  $2028,Y
6E1C: EE 17 6E     70              INC  DATA+1
6E1F: 18           71   BACK       CLC
6E20: A9 04        72              LDA  #$04
6E22: 6D 1B 6E     73              ADC  LOCATION+2
6E25: 8D 1B 6E     74              STA  LOCATION+2
6E28: EE 00 03     75              INC  $300
6E2B: AD 00 03     76              LDA  $300
6E2E: C9 08        77              CMP  #$08
6E30: D0 E4        78              BNE  DATA
6E32: EE 02 03     79              INC  $302
6E35: A2 00        80              LDX  #$00
6E37: 8E 00 03     81              STX  $300
6E3A: A2 20        82   HIGH       LDX  #$20
6E3C: 8E 1B 6E     83              STX  LOCATION+2
6E3F: 18           84              CLC
6E40: AD 1A 6E     85              LDA  LOCATION+1
6E43: 69 80        86              ADC  #$80
6E45: 8D 1A 6E     87              STA  LOCATION+1
```

```
6E48: B0 22        88              BCS   SET
6E4A: AE 02 03     89              LDX   $302
6E4D: E0 05        90              CPX   #$05
6E4F: D0 C5        91              BNE   DATA
6E51: EE 18 6E     92    OVER      INC   DATA+2
6E54: A2 28        93              LDX   #$28
6E56: 8E 1A 6E     94              STX   LOCATION+1
6E59: A2 20        95              LDX   #$20
6E5B: 8E 1B 6E     96              STX   LOCATION+2
6E5E: 8E 3B 6E     97              STX   HIGH+1
6E61: A2 00        98              LDX   #$00
6E63: 8E 00 03     99              STX   $300
6E66: 8E 02 03     100             STX   $302
6E69: 4C 75 6E     101             JMP   SET2
6E6C: EE 1B 6E     102   SET       INC   LOCATION+2
6E6F: EE 3B 6E     103             INC   HIGH+1
6E72: 4C 16 6E     104             JMP   DATA
6E75: AD 21 03     105   SET2      LDA   $321
6E78: 8D 17 6E     106             STA   DATA+1
6E7B: C8           107             INY
6E7C: C0 17        108             CPY   #$17
6E7E: D0 96        109             BNE   DATA
6E80: 20 58 FC     110             JSR   $FC58
6E83: A2 14        111   TEXT      LDX   #20
6E85: 86 25        112             STX   $25
6E87: A2 00        113             LDX   #0
6E89: BD 97 6E     114   TXT1      LDA   INFO,X
6E8C: C9 FF        115             CMP   #$FF
6E8E: F0 4D        116             BEQ   INPUT
6E90: 20 F0 FD     117             JSR   $FDF0
6E93: E8           118             INX
6E94: 4C 89 6E     119             JMP   TXT1
6E97: 8D           120   INFO      HEX   8D
6E98: A0 A0 A0
6E9B: A0 A0 A0
6E9E: A0 A0 A0
6EA1: A0 A0 A0
6EA4: A0 A0 A0
6EA7: A0 A0 C9     121             ASC   "              I"
6EAA: 8D           122             HEX   8D
6EAB: A0 A0 A0
```

23

```
6EAE: A0 A0 A0
6EB1: A0 A0 A0
6EB4: A0 CD EF
6EB7: F6 E5 BA
6EBA: A0 CA AB
6EBD: CC A0 A0
6EC0: A0 A0 D1
6EC3: F5 E9 F4
6EC6: BA A0 D1    123              ASC    "Move: J+L    Quit: Q"
6EC9: 8D          124              HEX    8D
6ECA: A0 A0 A0
6ECD: A0 A0 A0
6ED0: A0 A0 A0
6ED3: A0 A0 A0
6ED6: A0 A0 A0
6ED9: A0 A0 CB    125              ASC    "              K"
6EDC: FF          126              HEX    FF
6EDD: A2 12       127   INPUT      LDX    #18
6EDF: 86 25       128              STX    $25
6EE1: 20 1A FC    129              JSR    $FC1A
6EE4: 20 1B FD    130              JSR    $FD1B
6EE7: C9 C9       131              CMP    #$C9
6EE9: F0 1D       132              BEQ    UP
6EEB: C9 CB       133              CMP    #$CB
6EED: F0 3E       134              BEQ    DOWN
6EEF: C9 CA       135              CMP    #$CA
6EF1: F0 5F       136              BEQ    LEFT
6EF3: C9 CC       137              CMP    #$CC
6EF5: F0 07       138              BEQ    GORIGHT
6EF7: C9 D1       139              CMP    #$D1
6EF9: F0 06       140              BEQ    QUIT
6EFB: 4C 83 6E    141              JMP    TEXT
6EFE: 20 74 6F    142   GORIGHT    JSR    RIGHT
6F01: 20 2F FB    143   QUIT       JSR    $FB2F
6F04: 20 58 FC    144              JSR    $FC58
6F07: 60          145              RTS
6F08: AD 10 03    146   UP         LDA    $310
6F0B: C9 00       147              CMP    #$00
6F0D: F0 CE       148              BEQ    INPUT
6F0F: CE 10 03    149              DEC    $310
6F12: AD 21 03    150              LDA    $321
```

24

6F15: 8D 17 6E	151		STA DATA+1
6F18: AD 20 03	152		LDA $320
6F1B: 8D 18 6E	153		STA DATA+2
6F1E: 38	154		SEC
6F1F: AD 17 6E	155		LDA DATA+1
6F22: E9 08	156		SBC #$08
6F24: 8D 17 6E	157		STA DATA+1
6F27: 8D 21 03	158		STA $321
6F2A: 4C FF 6D	159		JMP CHECK
6F2D: AD 10 03	160	DOWN	LDA $310
6F30: C9 06	161		CMP #06
6F32: F0 A9	162		BEQ INPUT
6F34: EE 10 03	163		INC $310
6F37: AD 21 03	164		LDA $321
6F3A: 8D 17 6E	165		STA DATA+1
6F3D: AD 20 03	166		LDA $320
6F40: 8D 18 6E	167		STA DATA+2
6F43: 18	168		CLC
6F44: AD 17 6E	169		LDA DATA+1
6F47: 69 08	170		ADC #$08
6F49: 8D 17 6E	171		STA DATA+1
6F4C: 8D 21 03	172		STA $321
6F4F: 4C FF 6D	173		JMP CHECK
6F52: AD 11 03	174	LEFT	LDA $311
6F55: C9 00	175		CMP #$00
6F57: F0 18	176		BEQ BRANCH
6F59: CE 11 03	177		DEC $311
6F5C: AD 20 03	178		LDA $320
6F5F: 8D 18 6E	179		STA DATA+2
6F62: AD 21 03	180		LDA $321
6F65: 8D 17 6E	181		STA DATA+1
6F68: CE 18 6E	182		DEC DATA+2
6F6B: CE 20 03	183		DEC $320
6F6E: 4C FF 6D	184		JMP CHECK
6F71: 4C 83 6E	185	BRANCH	JMP TEXT
6F74: AD 11 03	186	RIGHT	LDA $311
6F77: C9 08	187		CMP #$08
6F79: F0 F6	188		BEQ BRANCH
6F7B: EE 11 03	189		INC $311
6F7E: AD 20 03	190		LDA $320
6F81: 8D 18 6E	191		STA DATA+2

25

```
6F84: AD 21 03    192         LDA   $321
6F87: 8D 17 6E    193         STA   DATA+1
6F8A: EE 18 6E    194         INC   DATA+2
6F8D: EE 20 03    195         INC   $320
6F90: 4C FF 6D    196         JMP   CHECK
```

--END ASSEMBLY--

ERRORS: 0

659 BYTES

SYMBOL TABLE - ALPHABETICAL ORDER:

?	BACK	=$6E1F		BLAH	=$6D65
	BRANCH	=$6F71		CHECK	=$6DFF
	DATA	=$6E16		DOWN	=$6F2D
	GORIGHT	=$6EFE		HIGH	=$6E3A
	INFO	=$6E97		INFO2	=$6D6D
	INFO3	=$6D79		INFO4	=$6D8E
	INFO5	=$6D9F		INFO6	=$6DC3
	INPUT	=$6EDD		LD2	=$6D06
	LD3	=$6D19		LD4	=$6D2C
	LD5	=$6D3F		LD6	=$6D52
	LEFT	=$6F52		LOCATION	=$6E19
?	OVER	=$6E51		QUIT	=$6F01
	RGB	=$6DDF		RIGHT	=$6F74
	SET	=$6E6C		SET2	=$6E75
	TEXT	=$6E83		TEXT2	=$6D03
	TEXT3	=$6D16		TEXT4	=$6D29
	TEXT5	=$6D3C		TEXT6	=$6D4F
	TXT1	=$6E89		UP	=$6F08

SYMBOL TABLE - NUMERICAL ORDER:

	TEXT2	=$6D03		LD2	=$6D06
	TEXT3	=$6D16		LD3	=$6D19
	TEXT4	=$6D29		LD4	=$6D2C
	TEXT5	=$6D3C		LD5	=$6D3F
	TEXT6	=$6D4F		LD6	=$6D52
	BLAH	=$6D65		INFO2	=$6D6D
	INFO3	=$6D79		INFO4	=$6D8E
	INFO5	=$6D9F		INFO6	=$6DC3
	RGB	=$6DDF		CHECK	=$6DFF
	DATA	=$6E16		LOCATION	=$6E19
?	BACK	=$6E1F		HIGH	=$6E3A
?	OVER	=$6E51		SET	=$6E6C
	SET2	=$6E75		TEXT	=$6E83
	TXT1	=$6E89		INFO	=$6E97
	INPUT	=$6EDD		GORIGHT	=$6EFE
	QUIT	=$6F01		UP	=$6F08
	DOWN	=$6F2D		LEFT	=$6F52
	BRANCH	=$6F71		RIGHT	=$6F74

After assembling the program in *Big Mac* as "MOTHERBOARD ASM", I wrote a simple BASIC program to merge it with the "MOTHERBOARD PICTURE" so it would all be self-contained as one BRUNable file.

My complete, merged program "MOTHERBOARD SIMULATION" has an entry point of $5FFD, which is a single line: JMP $6D00. Then the picture data runs from $6000 to $6CFF, followed by the actual code from $6D00 to $6FD2.

In order to demonstrate this, the following BASIC program BLOADs the assembled executable "MOTHERBOARD ASM", BLOADs the "MOTHERBOARD PICTURE", POKEs $4C $00 $6D into $5FFD, and BSAVEs the entire package under a different name as "MOTHERBOARD IIE DEMO".

```
1   REM   * MOTHERBOARD MERGER *
2   REM   *** BY BRIAN WISER ***
3   REM
4   REM
10  TEXT : HOME : HTAB 7: PRINT "IIe MOTHERBOARD
    MERGER DEMO": HTAB 6: PRINT "--------------------
    ---------"
20  VTAB 4: PRINT "This demonstration program will
    merge"
21  VTAB 5: PRINT "two files: (1) the assembled Big
    Mac"
22  VTAB 6: PRINT "source code for the IIe Motherboard
23  VTAB 7: PRINT "Simulation called 'MOTHERBOARD
    ASM'"
24  VTAB 8: PRINT "and (2) 'MOTHERBOARD PICTURE'"
25  VTAB 9: PRINT "into one BRUNable file called"
26  VTAB 10: PRINT "'MOTHERBOARD IIE DEMO'"
30  REM
40  PRINT CHR$(4);"BLOAD MOTHERBOARD ASM,A$6D00"
50  PRINT CHR$(4);"BLOAD MOTHERBOARD PICTURE,A$6000"
60  POKE 24573,76:  POKE 24574,0:  POKE 24575,109
70  PRINT CHR$(4);"BSAVE MOTHERBOARD IIE
    DEMO,A$5FFD,L4053"
80  REM
90  VTAB 22: HTAB 1: PRINT "MOTHERBOARD IIE DEMO was
    saved.":END
```

Lo-Res Horizontal Line

While not the most exciting program in the world, learning how to draw a low-resolution line in machine language is a good place to start exploring the world of **CALL -151** and the *Big Mac* assembler. In fact, the program is so complex that you need to **BRUN** it from the prompt, instead of using the included "H" startup program.

```
                    1    ORG   $6D00
6D00: 20 58 FC      2    JSR   $FC58
6D03: 20 40 FB      3    JSR   $FB40
6D06: A9 99         4    LDA   #$99
6D08: 85 30         5    STA   $30
6D0A: EA            6    NOP
6D0B: EA            7    NOP
6D0C: A0 01         8    LDY   #$01
6D0E: A2 1A         9    LDX   #$1A
6D10: 86 2C         10   STX   $2C
6D12: A9 05         11   LDA   #$05
6D14: 20 19 F8      12   JSR   $F819
6D17: 60            13   RTS
```

29

Annual Graph Matrix

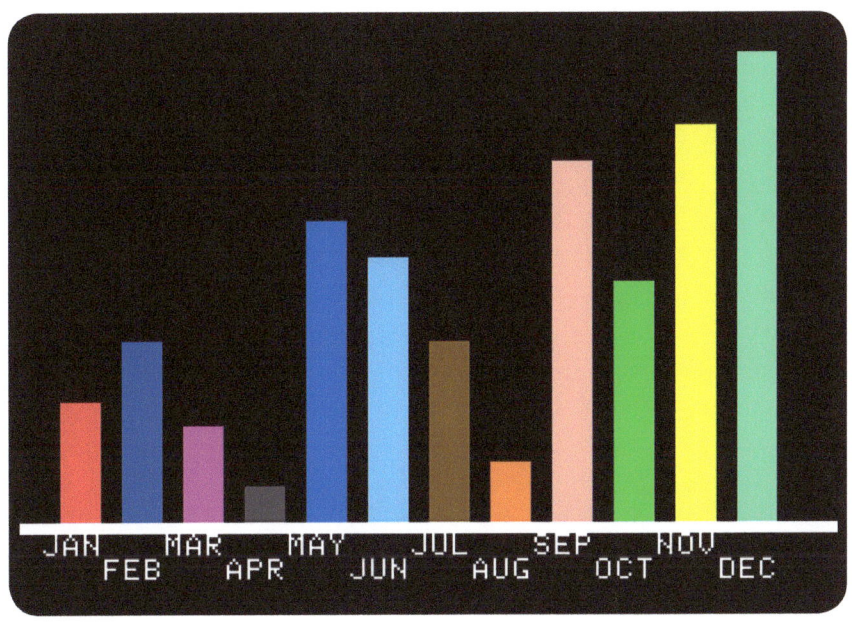

This program produces bar graph that shows monthly amounts for one year. Programmed with low-resolution graphics, it's both pretty and surprisingly useful. The POKE 34,6 prevents the top six lines of the text screen from being overwritten as an INPUT for each month that is displayed.

```
1  REM  * ANNUAL GRAPH MATRIX *
2  REM  *** BY BRIAN WISER ****
3  REM
4  REM
10  TEXT : HOME : HTAB 11: PRINT "ANNUAL GRAPH
    MATRIX": HTAB 10: PRINT "---------------------"
12  VTAB 5: PRINT "This program produces a bar graph
    that": VTAB 6: PRINT "shows monthly amounts for
    one year."
```

```
14   POKE 34,6: DIM A(12),B(12):A = 1: FOR B = 1 TO 12:
     READ A$
16   VTAB 9: PRINT "Amount for ";A$;: INPUT ": ";A(B):
     HOME : IF A < A(B)  THEN  LET A = A(B)
20   NEXT B: FOR B = 1 TO 12:B(B) = A(B) * 39 / A:
     NEXT B: DATA   January,February,March,April,
     May,June,July,August,September,October,November,
     December
25   HOME : VTAB 21: PRINT " JAN    MAR    MAY    JUL
     SEP    NOV": PRINT "    FEB    APR    JUN    AUG    OCT
     DEC": GR : COLOR= 15: HLIN 0,39 AT 39:C = 1: FOR
     B = 1 TO 12:D = D + 2: COLOR= C
30   C = C + 1: IF C = 4 THEN C = 5
40   IF C = 0 THEN C = 1
50   IF C = 10 THEN C = 11
60   IF C = 15 THEN C = 1
70   VLIN 38,39 - B(B) AT D: VLIN 38,39 - B(B) AT D +
     1:D = D + 1: NEXT B: VTAB 24: PRINT "Do you want
     to plot another graph? ";
80   GET A$: IF A$ = "Y" OR A$ = "y" THEN  CLEAR :
     GOTO 10
90   IF A$ = "N" OR A$ = "n" OR A$ = CHR$ (13) THEN
     TEXT : HOME : END
100   GOTO 80
```

Compound Interest

```
COMPOUND INTEREST
-------------------

Amount Invested: $1000
Interest Rate: 13.5
Number of Years: 5
```

Investment interest is calculated over time with this tool. Simply enter the amount invested, interest rate, and number of years that interest will be calculated.

Compounding periods of Annually, Semi Annually, Quarterly, and Daily are available to choose from. After seeing each of the interest earnings for your compounding period, a summary screen is presented:

```
Beginning Principal
Total Earned
Interest Earned
```

```
1    REM   ** COMPOUND INTEREST **
2    REM   **** BY BRIAN WISER ***
3    REM
4    REM
8    ONERR  GOTO 10
10   TEXT : HOME : HTAB 12: PRINT "COMPOUND INTEREST":
     HTAB 11: PRINT "--------------------"
12   VTAB 5: INPUT "Amount Invested: $";P: VTAB 7:
     INPUT "Interest Rate: ";I: VTAB 9: INPUT "Number
     of Years: ";N: HOME : HTAB 11: PRINT "COMPOUNDING
     PERIODS"
20   HTAB 10: PRINT "---------------------": VTAB 5:
     HTAB 3: PRINT "1 - Annually": PRINT : HTAB 3:
     PRINT "2 - Semi Annually": PRINT : HTAB 3: PRINT
     "3 - Quarterly"
25   PRINT : HTAB 3: PRINT "4 - Daily": PRINT :
     VTAB 14: PRINT "Option: ";: GET A: ON A GOTO
     30,40,50,60
30   X = 1: GOTO 70
40   X = 2: GOTO 70
50   X = 4: GOTO 70
60   X = 220: GOTO 70
70   I = I / X:N = N * X: HOME : PRINT "# AMOUNT":
     PRINT "_____":
     POKE 34,3: FOR Y = 1 TO N:A = P * (1 + I / 100) ^
     Y:A =  INT ((A + .005) * 100) / 100: IF Y / 19 =
     INT (Y / 19) THEN 140
80   PRINT Y;"-$";: PRINT A: NEXT Y: PRINT "_____
     _____": PRINT : VTAB 24:
     PRINT "Press any key to see results...";: GET A$
90   TEXT : HOME : PRINT "Beginning Principal: $";P:
     PRINT : PRINT "Total Earned: $";A: PRINT : PRINT
     "Interest Earned: $";A - P: VTAB 24: PRINT "Do you
     want to quit? ";
100  GET A$
110  IF A$ = "Y" OR A$ = "y" THEN  TEXT : HOME : END
120  IF A$ = "N" OR A$ = "n" THEN 10
130  GOTO 100
140  PRINT : PRINT "Press any key to continue...";:
     GET B$: HOME : GOTO 80
```

States & Capitals

```
            STATES & CAPITALS
            ------------------
This program is a tutorial to learn the
U.S. states and their capitals.

   1 - List of States & Capitals

   2 - Find a State or Capital

   3 - Guess a State

   4 - Guess a Capital

   5 - Quit

Option:
```

The U.S. states and capitals are something that every person should know and this is a great way to remember them. Typing the names into the program is also a good first step toward learning them. The program teaches the basics of **INPUT** and **DATA** statements.

```
1  REM  ** STATES & CAPITALS **
2  REM  *** BY BRIAN WISER ****
3  REM
4  REM
10  ONERR  GOTO 30
20  C = 1:D =  INT ((E * 100) / C): LET F = 0:G =
    0: DIM B$(51),C$(51): FOR A = 1 TO 50: READ
    B$(A),C$(A): NEXT A
30  TEXT : HOME : HTAB 12: PRINT "STATES & CAPITALS":
    HTAB 11: PRINT "-------------------"
32  VTAB 4: PRINT "This program is a tutorial to learn
    the U.S. states and their capitals."
```

```
34   VTAB 8: HTAB 3: PRINT "1 - List of States &
     Capitals": VTAB 10: HTAB 3: PRINT "2 - Find a
     State or Capital": VTAB 12: HTAB 3: PRINT "3 -
     Guess a State"
40   VTAB 14: HTAB 3: PRINT "4 - Guess a Capital":
     VTAB 16: HTAB 3: PRINT "5 - Quit": PRINT : PRINT
44   PRINT "Option: ";: GET H: ON H GOTO
     50,90,160,230,300
45   REM
46   REM   ===================
47   REM   LIST STATES/CAPITALS
48   REM   ===================
49   REM
50   HOME : HTAB 5: INVERSE : PRINT "STATES";: HTAB 22:
     PRINT "CAPITALS": NORMAL
55   VTAB 2: PRINT "_____
     ____": PRINT : POKE 34,3: LET I = 0: FOR A = 1 TO
     50: HTAB 5: PRINT B$(A);: HTAB 22: PRINT C$(A):
     LET I = I + 1: IF I = 18 THEN 80
60   IF I = 36 THEN 80
70   NEXT A: VTAB 24: PRINT "Press any key to
     continue...";: GET A$: TEXT : HOME : GOTO 30
80   VTAB 24: PRINT "Press any key to continue...";:
     GET A$: HOME : GOTO 70
85   REM
86   REM   ===================
87   REM   FIND STATES/CAPITALS
88   REM   ===================
89   REM
90   HOME : INPUT "Type a State or Capital: ";D$: IF D$
     = "" THEN   HOME : GOTO 30
100  FOR B = 1 TO 50: IF D$ = B$(B) THEN  GOTO 140
110  IF D$ = C$(B) THEN   GOTO 150
120  NEXT B
130  VTAB 24: HTAB 1: PRINT "Press any key to
     continue...";: GET E$: GOTO 90
140  VTAB 4: PRINT "Its Capital is ";: INVERSE : PRINT
     C$(B);: NORMAL : GOTO 130
150  VTAB 4: PRINT "Its State is ";: INVERSE : PRINT
     B$(B);: NORMAL : GOTO 130
155  REM
```

```
156  REM  ====================
157  REM      GUESS A STATE
158  REM  ====================
159  REM
160  GOSUB 310
170  GOSUB 340: HOME : PRINT "What is ";C$(J);"'s
     state? ";: INPUT "";F$: IF F$ = "" THEN  GOTO 190
180  C = C + 1: GOTO 200
190  HOME : GOSUB 320: VTAB 2: PRINT "Score:";: HTAB
     11: PRINT E" correct": PRINT: PRINT "Out of:";:
     HTAB 11: PRINT C" ";"tries": PRINT: PRINT "Which
     is:";: HTAB 11: PRINT D;"% accurate"
195  VTAB 24: PRINT "Press any key to continue...";:
     GET A$: HOME : GOTO 30
200  IF F$ = B$(J) THEN  GOTO 220
210  PRINT : PRINT : PRINT "The answer is ";: INVERSE
     : PRINT B$(J): NORMAL : VTAB 24: PRINT "Press any
     key to continue...";: GET A$: GOTO 170
220  PRINT : PRINT : PRINT "Correct!":E = E + 1: VTAB
     24: PRINT "Press any key to continue...";: GET
     A$: GOTO 170
225  REM
226  REM  ====================
227  REM      GUESS A CAPITAL
228  REM  ====================
229  REM
230  GOSUB 310
240  GOSUB 340: HOME : PRINT "What is ";B$(J);"'s
     capital? ";: INPUT "";F$: IF F$ = "" THEN
     GOTO 260
250  C = C + 1: GOTO 270
260  HOME : GOSUB 320: VTAB 2: PRINT "Score:";: HTAB
     11: PRINT E" correct": PRINT: PRINT "Out of:";:
     HTAB 11: PRINT C" ";"tries": PRINT: PRINT "Which
     is:";: HTAB 11: PRINT D;"% accurate"
265  VTAB 24: PRINT "Press any key to continue...";:
     GET A$: HOME : GOTO 30
270  IF F$ = C$(J) THEN  GOTO 290
280  PRINT : PRINT "The answer is ";: INVERSE : PRINT
     C$(J): NORMAL : VTAB 24: PRINT "Press any key to
     continue...";: GET A$: GOTO 240
```

```
290  PRINT : PRINT "Correct!":E = E + 1: VTAB 24:
     PRINT "Press any key to continue...";: GET A$:
     GOTO 240
300  HOME : END
305  REM
306  REM  ====================
307  REM      SUBROUTINES
308  REM  ====================
309  REM
310  J = 0:E = 0:C = 0: RETURN
320  IF C = 0 THEN C = 1
330  D =  INT ((E * 100) / C): RETURN
340  J =  INT ( RND (1) * 50) + 1: RETURN
345  REM
350  DATA  ALABAMA, MONTGOMERY, ALASKA, JUNEAU,
     ARIZONA, PHOENIX, ARKANSAS, LITTLE ROCK,
     CALIFORNIA, SACRAMENTO, COLORADO, DENVER
355  DATA  CONNECTICUT, HARTFORD, DELAWARE, DOVER,
     FLORIDA, TALLAHASSEE, GEORGIA, ATLANTA, HAWAII,
     HONOLULU, IDAHO, BOISE
360  DATA  ILLINOIS, SPRINGFIELD, INDIANA,
     INDIANAPOLIS, IOWA, DES MOINES, KANSAS, TOPEKA,
     KENTUCKY, FRANKFORT, LOUISIANA, BATON ROUGE
365  DATA  MAINE, AUGUSTA, MARYLAND, ANNAPOLIS,
     MASSACHUSETTS, BOSTON, MICHIGAN, LANSING,
     MINNESOTA, ST. PAUL
370  DATA  MISSISSIPPI, JACKSON, MISSOURI, JEFFERSON
     CITY, MONTANA, HELENA, NEBRASKA, LINCOLN, NEVADA,
     CARSON CITY, NEW HAMPSHIRE, CONCORD
375  DATA  NEW JERSEY, TRENTON, NEW MEXICO, SANTA FE,
     NEW YORK, ALBANY, NORTH CAROLINA, RALEIGH
380  DATA  NORTH DAKOTA, BISMARK, OHIO, COLUMBUS,
     OKLAHOMA, OKLAHOMA CITY, OREGON, SALEM,
     PENNSYLVANIA, HARRISBURG, RHODE ISLAND,
     PROVIDENCE
385  DATA  SOUTH CAROLINA, COLUMBIA, SOUTH DAKOTA,
     PIERRE, TENNESSEE, NASHVILLE, TEXAS, AUSTIN
390  DATA  UTAH, SALT LAKE CITY, VERMONT, MONTPELIER,
     VIRGINIA, RICHMOND, WASHINGTON, OLYMPIA, WEST
     VIRGINIA, CHARLESTON, WISCONSIN, MADISON,
     WYOMING, CHEYENNE
```

Access Code

```
ENTER ACCESS CODE: ▩
```

    This is a fun little password program that sounds an alarm if the correct password is not entered, along with "ACCESS DENIED." If it is set as the startup HELLO program on your disk, entering the correct password will run your favorite HELLO program – in this case my "H" program on line 150.

    In an attempt at greater security, the password starts with "6" (line 110) and ends with "APPLE" (line 170). To choose a different password, set the length in line 60 and update line 170. In order to prevent casual listing, the Reset key is disabled and the program is cleared from memory after entering the correct password.

```
1   REM   ***** ACCESS CODE *****
2   REM   **** BY BRIAN WISER ***
3   REM
4   REM
8   ONERR  GOTO 160
10   FOR X = 0 TO 17: READ A: POKE 12345 + X,A: NEXT :
     DATA    173,48,192,136,208,4,198,0,240,7,202,208,
     246,166,0,208,239,96
30   POKE 1010,102: POKE 1011,213: POKE 1012,112
40   HOME : VTAB 12: HTAB 1: PRINT "ENTER ACCESS CODE:
     ";
50   GET N
60   FOR B = 1 TO 5
70   GET A$(B)
80   READ CD$(B): IF A$(B) <  > CD$(B) THEN  GOTO 160
90   NEXT B
100   IF A$(B) = CD$(B) THEN 110
110   IF N <  > 6 THEN 160
120   POKE 1010,191 : POKE 1011,157 : POKE 1012,56
150   PRINT : PRINT  CHR$ (4);"RUN H": NEW
160   HOME : INVERSE : VTAB 12: HTAB 14: PRINT "ACCESS
      DENIED": POKE 45623,234: POKE 44503,234: FOR Z =
      1 TO 1000000: CALL 12345: NEXT Z: NEW
170   DATA  A,P,P,L,E
```

```
DISK VOLUME 254 311 FREE SECTORS = 80K
 A [A] H
*A [B] THE ETCH-A-SKETCH
 B [C] INVERT
*A [D] THE APPLE
*B [E] MOTHERBOARD SIMULATION
 B [F] MOTHERBOARD SIMULATION.s
 A [G] MOTHERBOARD MERGER
 B [H] MOTHERBOARD ASM
 B [I] MOTHERBOARD PICTURE
 B [J] LORES HORIZONTAL LINE
 B [K] LORES HORIZONTAL LINE.s
*A [L] ANNUAL GRAPH MATRIX
*A [M] COMPOUND INTEREST
*A [N] STATES & CAPITALS
*A [O] ACCESS CODE
*A [P] RANDOM ACCESS FILER
*A [Q] TUNNEL RACE
*A [R] THE AUTOBAHN
*A [S] JOYSTICK CALIBRATION

Type letter to run, or 1-Load, 2-Lock,
```

A good HELLO startup program was a very useful thing for accessing programs on one's disks, and "H" was a neat one that I found and updated. I changed fully capitalized words to title case, and added some commands and design improvements.

While it was written for 40 columns and DOS 3.3, it's still one of my favorites. And I suppose my friends found it useful too, as my version started to appear on disks throughout the computer lab.

By design, it will only display files that are LOCKed. Many of my disks contained data files that I didn't want to see on the launch screen because they couldn't be run directly. Thus, the simplicity of having only locked files display. However, to leave options available, choosing "0 - Normal Catalog" or "7 - Space on Disk" will display all the files. All the options are:

Type a letter corresponding to a file to RUN or BRUN, or:

```
        1 – Load
        2 – Lock
        3 – Unlock
        4 – Delete
        5 – Rename
        6 – Verify
        7 – Space on Disk
        8 – Catalog
        9 – Initialize Disk
        0 – Normal Catalog
    SPACE – Exit
```

```
1  REM   *******   H   ********
2  REM   *****  ENHANCED  *****
3  REM   *** BY BRIAN WISER ***
4  REM
5  REM   Displays Locked Files
6  REM   "0" Displays All Files
7  REM
8  REM
10  ONERR  GOTO 390
20  POKE 44513,67: FOR D = 790 TO 891: READ E: POKE
    D,E: NEXT D: DATA  169,0,141,121,3,141,122,3,133,
    76,32,227,3,132,28,133,29,169,2,133,77,169,0,160,
    3,145,28,160,5,145,28,169,17,136,145,28,165,76,16
    0,8,145,28,165,77,200,145,28,160
30  DATA 12,169,1,145,28,169,0,200,145,28,32,227,3,32,
    217,3,160,13,177,28,240,3,76,45,255,160,56,177,76
    ,162,7,10,144,8,238,121,3,208,3,238,122,3,202,16,
    242,200,192,196,144,233,96,0,0,0: POKE 889,1
40  TEXT : HOME :C$ =  CHR$ (4): PRINT C$;"CATALOG":
    B =  PEEK (37) - 2: IF B > 22 THEN B = 22
50  F = 0:G = 0
60  H = 0:I = 4: FOR J = 4 TO 23: GOSUB 360: IF C <  >
    160 THEN  POKE L - 1,219: POKE L,H + 193: POKE L
    + 1,221:H = H + 1:M = J
```

```
70    NEXT J: VTAB 24:A$ = "Type letter to run, or
      1-Load, 2-Lock, 3-Unlock, 4-Delete, 5-Rename,
      6-Verify, 7-Space on Disk, 8-Catalog,
      9-Initialize Disk, 0-Normal Catalog, SPACE-
      Exit................"
80    POKE  - 16368,0
90    POKE 44513,2:B$ = "RUN": HTAB 1: PRINT  LEFT$
      (A$,39);:A$ =  MID$ (A$,2) +  LEFT$ (A$,1):K =
      PEEK ( - 16384): IF K = 160 THEN 440
100   IF K < 129 THEN  FOR K = 1 TO 74: NEXT :K =
      FRE (0): GOTO 90
110   IF K = 176 THEN  GOTO 460
120   IF K = 160 THEN 440
130   POKE  - 16383,0:K = K - 176: IF K < 1 THEN 290
140   HTAB 1: CALL  - 868: IF K < 1 THEN 440
150   IF K = 7 THEN 380
160   IF K = 8 THEN 390
170   IF K = 9 THEN 410
180   IF K < 1 OR K > 42 THEN 440
190   IF K > 0 AND K < 7 THEN 210
200   GET D$:K =  ASC (D$) - 48:B$ = "RUN": POKE
      44513,2: GOTO 290
210   PRINT "Press 'Letter' to ";: IF K = 1 THEN B$ =
      "LOAD": POKE 44513,2
220   IF K = 2 THEN B$ = "LOCK"
230   IF K = 3 THEN B$ = "UNLOCK"
240   IF K = 4 THEN B$ = "DELETE"
250   IF K = 5 THEN B$ = "RENAME"
260   IF K = 6 THEN B$ = "VERIFY"
270   SPEED= 255: INVERSE : IF K = 5 THEN F = 1
280   PRINT B$;: GET D$: NORMAL: GET D$:K= ASC (D$) - 48
290   IF K < 17 OR K > H + 16 THEN 90
300   I = 1:J = M - H + K - 16: GOSUB 360: IF C = 212
      AND B$ = "RUN" THEN B$ = "EXEC": POKE 44513,2
310   IF C = 194 AND (B$ = "RUN" OR B$ = "LOAD") THEN
      B$ = "B" + B$: POKE 44513,2
320   IF B$ = "EXEC" THEN G = 1: POKE 44513,2
330   FOR I = 6 TO 39: GOSUB 360:B$ = B$ +  CHR$ (C):
      NEXT : HTAB 1: CALL  - 868: IF F = 1 THEN 370
340   PRINT B$: PRINT C$;B$: IF G = 1 THEN  END
350   GOTO 40
```

```
360  N =  INT (J / 8):O = J - N * 8:L = 1024 + 128 * O
     + 40 * N + I:C =  PEEK (L): RETURN
370  POKE  - 16368,0: INPUT "New Name: ";E$: PRINT
     C$;B$;",";E$: GOTO 390
380  PRINT C$;"NOMON C,I,O": HOME: PRINT C$;"CATALOG":
     POKE 33,40: POKE 34,0
385  VTAB 3: HTAB 17: CALL -868: CALL 790: POKE
     216,0:A = PEEK (889) + PEEK (890) * 256:K =  INT
     (A * .256 + .5): INVERSE : VTAB 3: HTAB 17: PRINT
     A;" FREE SECTORS = ";K;"K": NORMAL : VTAB 24:
     GOTO 60
390  POKE 44513,67
400  PRINT C$;"NOMON C,I,O": HOME: PRINT C$;"CATALOG":
     GOTO 50
410  POKE - 16368,0: HTAB 1: CALL -868: INPUT "Volume
     Number: ";P: HTAB 1: CALL  -868: HOME : VTAB 11:
     HTAB 5: PRINT "Insert Disk to be Initialized":
     PRINT : HTAB 11: PRINT "and press a key..."
420  F =  PEEK ( - 16384): IF F < 128 THEN 420
430  POKE  - 16368,0: PRINT C$;"INIT H,V";P: GOTO 390
440  IF K <  > 160 THEN 80
450  POKE  - 16368,0: POKE 44513,2: HOME : NEW : END
460  POKE 44513,2: GOTO 400
```

Random Access Filer

```
     RANDOM ACCESS TEXT FILES
     ---------------------------

   1 - Create a Contacts file
   2 - Add records
   3 - Update records
   4 - List/Sort a file
   5 - Search a file
   6 - Delete records
   7 - Delete file
   8 - Catalog
   9 - Quit

OPTION:
```

With this very simple database program I learned how to create, view, and modify records in a text file. It stores names, addresses, and phone numbers. Its value is more educational than practical. Here's how to create, add, and view your contacts with examples:

1. Create a Contacts file

    File: FRIENDS
    Maximum Record Length: 50

2. Add Records

    File: FRIENDS
    Maximum Record Length: 50

    "There are 0 records in this file."

    First Record Number to Add: 1
    Last Record Number to Add: 3

45

In this example, the program will then ask for the name, address, and phone for records 1 to 3, then return to the menu.

```
3.  List/Sort a file

      File:  FRIENDS
      Maximum Record Length:  50

      Do you want to alphabetize the file?
      Print to (S)creen or (D)isk?
```

If Screen is chosen, then the records will be displayed, otherwise Disk will save a file. You can type a record number to view that person's name/address/phone, or press Return to go back to the menu.

```
    File:  FRIENDS
    There are 3 records in this file.
    --------------------------------
    1 - Woz
    2 - Steve
    3 - Ron
```

There are a few other options to explore, but that's essentially the program in all its glory. Enjoy!

```
1   REM   * RANDOM ACCESS FILER *
2   REM   *** BY BRIAN WISER ****
3   REM
4   REM
10  ONERR  GOTO 30
20  CLEAR : DIM B$(300): DIM C$(300): DIM
    E$(300),F$(300): TEXT : HOME :A = 700: LET D$ =
    CHR$ (4)
30  HOME : HTAB 9: PRINT "RANDOM ACCESS TEXT FILES":
    HTAB 8: PRINT "--------------------------"
35  VTAB 5: HTAB 3: PRINT "1 - Create a Contacts
    file": PRINT : HTAB 3: PRINT "2 - Add records":
    PRINT : HTAB 3: PRINT "3 - Update records": PRINT
    : HTAB 3: PRINT "4 - List/Sort a file": PRINT :
    HTAB 3
```

```
40   PRINT "5 - Search a file": PRINT : HTAB 3: PRINT
     "6 - Delete records": PRINT : HTAB 3: PRINT
     "7 - Delete file": PRINT : HTAB 3: PRINT "8 -
     Catalog": PRINT
45   HTAB 3: PRINT "9 - Quit": VTAB 24: PRINT "OPTION:
     ";: GET B: IF B < 1 OR B > 9 THEN 30
50   ON B GOSUB 80,170,110,220,180,350,90,70,450
60   TEXT : GOTO 30
70   HOME : PRINT : PRINT D$;"CATALOG": PRINT : PRINT
     "Press any key to return to menu...";: GET G$:
     GOTO 30
75   REM
76   REM   =======================
77   REM   CREATE, DELETE, UPDATE
78   REM   =======================
79   REM
80   HOME : HTAB 14: PRINT "CREATE FILE": HTAB 13:
     PRINT "-------------": GOSUB 460: GOSUB 480: GOSUB
     500: PRINT D$;"WRITE";H$;",R0": PRINT 0: PRINT
     D$;"WRITE";H$;",R1": PRINT "No files exist":
     GOSUB 510: RETURN
90   HOME : HTAB 14: PRINT "DELETE A FILE": HTAB 13:
     PRINT "---------------": GOSUB 460: VTAB 23: PRINT
     "Is this correct? ";: GET I$: IF I$ = "N" THEN
     HOME : GOTO 90
100  PRINT : PRINT D$;"DELETE";H$: RETURN
110  HOME : HTAB 13: PRINT "UPDATE RECORDS": HTAB 12:
     PRINT "----------------"
115  REM
116  REM   ====================
117  REM   MAIN RECORDS ROUTINE
118  REM   ====================
119  REM
120  GOSUB 460: GOSUB 480: GOSUB 500: GOSUB 520: GOSUB
     510
130  HOME : PRINT "There are ";: PRINT D;: PRINT "
     records in this file.": PRINT : PRINT : INPUT
     "First Record Number to Add: ";E: IF E > (D + 1)
     OR E = 0 THEN 130
140  PRINT : INPUT "Last Record Number to Add: ";F: IF
     F > D THEN G = F: GOTO 160
```

47

```
150  G = D
160  FOR H = E TO F: HOME : INVERSE : PRINT "RECORD
     #";H: NORMAL : PRINT : INPUT "Name: ";B$(H):
     INPUT "Address: ";J$(H): INPUT "Phone: ";K$(H):
     NEXT H: GOSUB 500
164  FOR H = E TO F: PRINT D$;"WRITE";H$;",R";H: PRINT
     B$(H): NEXT H: PRINT D$;"WRITE";H$;",R0": PRINT
     G: GOSUB 510: RETURN
165  REM
166  REM  =================
167  REM      ADD RECORDS
168  REM  =================
169  REM
170  HOME : HTAB 15: PRINT "ADD RECORDS": HTAB 14:
     PRINT "-------------": GOTO 120
175  REM
176  REM  =================
177  REM     SEARCH A FILE
178  REM  =================
179  REM
180  HOME : HTAB 15: PRINT "SEARCH FILE": HTAB 14:
     PRINT "-------------": GOSUB 460: GOSUB 480: HOME
     : INPUT "Name to Find: ";E$: GOSUB 500: PRINT
     D$;"READ";H$;",R0": INPUT D
185  FOR I = 1 TO D: PRINT D$;"READ";H$;",R";I: INPUT
     M$: IF M$ = E$ THEN  HOME : INVERSE : PRINT
     "RECORD #";I: NORMAL : PRINT : PRINT "NAME:
     ";M$:J = 1
190  NEXT I: IF J = 1 THEN J = 0: GOTO 210
200  K =  LEN (E$):C = (40 - K - 10) / 2: HOME :
     INVERSE : VTAB 11: HTAB C: PRINT E$;: NORMAL :
     PRINT " not found"
210  GOSUB 510: VTAB 24: PRINT "Press any key to
     return to menu...";: GET G$: RETURN
215  REM
216  REM  =================
217  REM  LIST / SORT A FILE
218  REM  =================
219  REM
220  HOME : HTAB 13: PRINT "LIST/SORT FILE": HTAB
     12: PRINT "----------------": GOSUB 460: GOSUB
```

```
480: GOSUB 500: GOSUB 520: FOR M = 1 TO D: PRINT
     D$;"READ";H$;",R";M: INPUT C$(M):F$(M) = C$(M):
     NEXT M: GOSUB 510
230  HOME : PRINT "Do you want to alphabetize the
     file? ";: GET I$: IF I$ = "N" OR I$ = "n" THEN
     290
240  IF I$ = "Y" OR I$ = "y" THEN 260
250  GOTO 230
260  VTAB 23: HTAB 12: PRINT "Alphabetizing";: FOR N =
     1 TO D
270  FOR O = N TO D: IF C$(N) > C$(O) THEN N$ =
     C$(N):C$(N) = C$(O):C$(O) = N$:N$ = "": GOTO 270
280  NEXT O: PRINT ".";: NEXT N
290  HOME : PRINT "Print to (S)creen or (D)isk? ";:
     GET G$: IF G$ = "D" OR G$ = "d" THEN 340
300  IF G$ = "S" OR G$ = "s" THEN 320
310  GOTO 290
320  HOME : PRINT "File: ";H$: PRINT : PRINT "There
     are ";D;" records in this file.": PRINT "-------
     --------------------------------"
325  FOR M = 1 TO D: PRINT M;" - ";: PRINT C$(M): IF M
     / 23 =  INT (M / 23) THEN  PRINT "Press any key
     to continue...";: GET G$
330  NEXT M: FOR P = 1 TO D:C$(P) = F$(P): NEXT P:
     VTAB 24: INPUT "Type number or press Return for
     menu: ";Q: HOME : PRINT B$(Q): PRINT J$(Q): PRINT
     K$(Q): VTAB 24: PRINT "Press any key to return to
     list...";: GET A$: GOTO 320
340  PRINT : GOSUB 500: FOR M = 1 TO D: PRINT
     D$;"WRITE";H$;",R";M: PRINT C$(M): NEXT M: GOSUB
     510: GOTO 30
345  REM
346  REM  ==================
347  REM     DELETE RECORDS
348  REM  ==================
349  REM
350  HOME : HTAB 13: PRINT "DELETE RECORDS": HTAB 12:
     PRINT "----------------": GOSUB 460: GOSUB 480:
     GOSUB 500: GOSUB 520: GOSUB 510: HOME : PRINT
     "There are ";D;" records in this file.": PRINT
```

```
355  PRINT "Type the names to be deleted and press
     Return when finished.": PRINT : PRINT :I = 0
360  I = I + 1: INPUT "Name: ";E$(I): IF E$(I) = ""
     THEN 380
370  PRINT : GOTO 360
380  IF I = 1 THEN 440
390  GOSUB 500: FOR R = 1 TO (I - 1): FOR M = 1 TO
     D: PRINT D$;"READ";H$;",R";M: INPUT C$: IF C$ =
     E$(R) THEN   GOSUB 410
400  NEXT M: NEXT R: PRINT D$;"WRITE";H$;",R0": PRINT
     D: GOSUB 510: GOTO 440
410  IF M = D THEN 430
420  FOR S = (M + 1) TO D: PRINT D$;"READ";H$;",R";S:
     INPUT N$: PRINT D$;"WRITE";H$;",R";S - 1: PRINT
     N$: NEXT S
430  D = D - 1: RETURN
440  RETURN
445  REM
446  REM  ==================
447  REM      ADD RECORDS
448  REM  ==================
449  REM
450  HOME : END
460  VTAB 5: HTAB 3: INPUT "File: ";H$: IF H$ = ""
     THEN H$ = O$: VTAB 5: HTAB 9: PRINT H$: RETURN
470  O$ = H$: RETURN
480  PRINT : HTAB 3: INPUT "Maximum Number of Records:
     ";L$:L =  VAL (L$): IF L$ = "" THEN L = T: VTAB
     7: HTAB 18: PRINT L: RETURN
490  T = L: RETURN
500  PRINT : PRINT D$;"OPEN";H$;",L";L: RETURN
510  PRINT : PRINT D$;"CLOSE";H$: RETURN
520  PRINT : PRINT D$;"READ";H$;",R0": INPUT D: RETURN
```

Tunnel Race

This is quite a fun text-based racing game that appeared in the computer lab one day. Of course, I had to make my usual enhancements including a new " | " character choice for the car and slashes indicating the direction. The object of the game is to get as far as you can in the tunnel without crashing. The controls are:

[J]	Left
[L]	Right
[I]	Slow down
[K]	Speed up
[SPACE]	go Straight

You can choose up to 99 cars and pick a custom keyboard character for the car. Pressing Return for the default car gives you an *. If you choose |, then it uses / and \ to show diagonal movement.

If you choose to have obstacles, then you can pick a skill level for the obstacles you'll encounter.

```
1    REM  **** TUNNEL RACE *****
2    REM  *****  ENHANCED  *****
3    REM  *** BY BRIAN WISER ***
4    REM
5    REM
10   ONERR  GOTO 20
20   CLEAR : DIM B(70),A(99)
30   TEXT : HOME : HTAB 15: PRINT "TUNNEL RACE": HTAB
     14: PRINT "-------------": VTAB 4: PRINT "The
     object of the game is to drive as   far as you can
     in the tunnel without   crashing. The controls
     are:"
35   VTAB 10: HTAB 10: PRINT "[J]  Left": VTAB 12: HTAB
     10: PRINT "[L]  Right": VTAB 14: HTAB 10: PRINT
     "[I]  Slow down"
40   VTAB 16: HTAB 10: PRINT "[K]  Speed up": VTAB 18:
     HTAB 10: PRINT "[SPACE]  go Straight": VTAB 24:
     PRINT "Press any key to continue...";: GET A$
50   PRINT : HOME : VTAB 11: HTAB 2: INPUT "How many
     cars do you want? (1-99): ";E$:D =  VAL (E$): IF
     D = 0 THEN D = 1
60   IF D > 99 OR D < 0 THEN 50
70   PRINT : HOME : VTAB 7: HTAB 13: PRINT "Default =
     *": VTAB 8: HTAB 13: PRINT "Cool    = |":
75   VTAB 11:  HTAB 10: PRINT "Character for Car: ";:
     GET C$: IF C$ =  CHR$ (13) THEN C$ = "*"
80   PRINT :E = 1: PRINT : HOME : VTAB 11: HTAB 9:
     PRINT "Do you want obstacles? ";: GET E$: IF E$ =
     CHR$ (13) THEN N = 0: GOTO 120
90   IF E$ = "Y" or E$ = "y" THEN N = 1
100   IF E$ = "N" or E$ = "n" THEN N = 0: GOTO 120
110   HOME : VTAB 11: HTAB 5: INPUT "Obstacle Skill
     Level (1-40): ";Q:R = Q: IF Q < 0 OR Q > 40 THEN
     110
120   S = 255: HOME : VTAB 11: PRINT "Press any key to
     begin the race...";: GET B$:B = 2
130   HOME : POKE 34,2: VTAB 1: PRINT "Score=": VTAB
     1: HTAB 27: PRINT "Cars Left=";D - G; SPC( 1):
     SPEED= S: HTAB 14: PRINT "Speed=";S:F = 0:G = G + 1
```

```
140  H = (H = 0) * 10 + H - .01 + (H < 3):I =  PEEK
     (49152):J = J - (I = 202) + (I = 204) + (J = 0) *
     10:K = (K < 4) * 2 + K +  SGN ( RND (1) - .5) -
     (K + H > 30): COLOR= B: HLIN 0,K - 1 AT 47: HLIN
     K + H + 1,39 AT 47
150  C =  SCRN( J - 1,21): HTAB (J - O):P =  INT ( RND
     (1) * R): IF N = 1 THEN  PLOT P,47
160  IF I = 128 +  ASC ("K") THEN S = S + 10: IF S >
     255 THEN S = 255
170  IF I = 128 +  ASC ("I") THEN S = S - 10: IF S < 0
     THEN S = 0
180  F$ = C$: IF C$ = "|" THEN  GOSUB 290
190  VTAB 11: PRINT F$;: IF E = 1 THEN A =  PEEK ( -
     16336)
200  SPEED= S: HTAB 36: VTAB 24: PRINT :F = F + 1:
     HTAB 7: VTAB 1: PRINT F - 13; SPC( 3): HTAB 20:
     PRINT S; SPC( 3): IF C <  > 2 THEN 140
210  SPEED= 255: PRINT "": FOR L = 0 TO 200: NEXT L
220  TEXT : HOME :A(G) = F - 13: PRINT "Your Score is:
     ";A(G): VTAB 3: PRINT "Cars Left: ";D - G: FOR L
     = 0 TO 1300: NEXT L: IF G = D THEN 240
230  GOTO 130
240  TEXT : HOME : PRINT "Car-Score": PRINT "--------
     -": FOR J = 1 TO D: IF (J / 18) =  INT (J / 18)
     THEN  GET D$
250  PRINT "[";J;"]";: HTAB 6: PRINT A(J):M = M +
     A(J): NEXT J: PRINT : PRINT : PRINT "Your total
     score is: ";M: VTAB 24: PRINT "Do you want to
     play again? ";
260  GET A$: IF A$ = "Y" OR A$ = "y" THEN  CLEAR :
     TEXT : GOTO 30
270  IF A$ = "N" OR A$ = "n" THEN  HOME : END
280  GOTO 260
290  F$ = C$: IF I = 202 THEN F$ = "/"
300  IF I = 204 THEN F$ = "\"
310  RETURN
```

The Autobahn

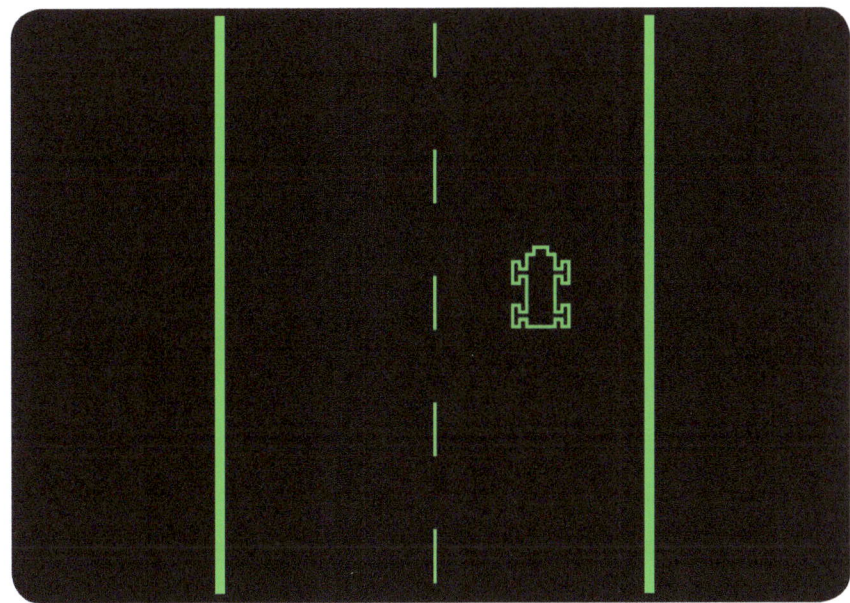

One of my fun programming assignments was to have even more fun and write a game in high-resolution graphics. The first thing that came to mind was a racing game and dodging oncoming cars, a bit like *Spy Hunter*. Like with all assignments, time was a factor.

I learned quite a bit about hi-res graphics and did my best given the time. The result is... almost a game. The car appears on the race track, the divider lines move, and the car can be controlled – but that's where the excitement ends. Perhaps I'll finish it someday. The controls are:

J - Left

L - Right

I - Speed Up

K - Brake

SPACE - Stop Motion

Q - Quit

55

```
10    REM   **** THE AUTOBAHN ****
20    REM   *** BY BRIAN WISER ***
30    REM
40    REM
50    HOME : HTAB 14: INVERSE : PRINT "THE AUTOBAHN":
      NORMAL
51    NORMAL : VTAB 4: PRINT "Welcome to the Autobahn!"
52    VTAB 6: PRINT "The Keys Used to Move Are:"
53    HTAB 8: VTAB 9: PRINT "J - Left": HTAB 8: VTAB 11:
      PRINT "L - Right": HTAB 8: VTAB 13: PRINT "I -
      Speed Up"
54    HTAB 8: VTAB 15: PRINT "K - Brake":HTAB 4:VTAB
      17: PRINT "SPACE - Stop Motion": HTAB 8: VTAB 19:
      PRINT "Q - Quit"
55    VTAB 24: PRINT "Press Any Key to Start the
      Race...";: GET A$: HOME
57    REM
58    REM   *** DRAW INITIAL TRACK ***
59    REM
60    HGR
65    SCALE= 1
70    HCOLOR= 3: RESTORE : FOR Z = 1 TO 6: READ A,B,C:
      HPLOT A,B TO A,C: NEXT Z
80    DATA    78,0,159,79,0,159,80,0,159,200,0,159,201,0,
      159,202,0,159
85    F = 1:G = 36:H = 71:I = 106:J = 141
90    GOSUB 210
94    XDRAW 1 AT 36,0
95    A1 = X:B1 = Y
96    X = 170:Y = 140
97    REM
98    REM   *** GET CONTROL KEY ***
99    REM
100   K = PEEK (-16384): IF K > 127 THEN K = K - 128:
      POKE -16368,0
102   REM
103   REM   *** DRAW MIDDLE LINES AND CAR ***
104   REM
105   GOSUB 1000
109   XDRAW 1 AT A1,B1
110   HCOLOR= 3
```

```
120   IF K = 73 OR K = 105 THEN Y = Y - 5:M = Y - 1:Z =
      Z + 1
130   IF K = 75 OR K = 107 THEN Y = Y + 5:M = Y + 1:Z =
      Z - 1
140   IF K = 74 OR K = 106 THEN X = X - 5:N = X - 1
150   IF K = 76 OR K = 108 THEN X = X + 5:N = X + 1
152   IF K = 81 OR K = 113 THEN  TEXT : HOME : END
155   IF Z = 0 THEN Z = 1
156   IF Z > 5 THEN Z = 5
160   ROT= 0
170   SCALE= 1
180   XDRAW 1 AT X,Y
181   IF X = 203 THEN  GOTO 3000
195   A1 = X:B1 = Y
196   GOSUB 1060
200   GOTO 100
210   S = 768
220   S1 =  INT (S / 256):S2 = S - S1 * 256
230   POKE 232,S2: POKE 233,S1
240   READ N:Q = N
250   POKE S,N: POKE S + 1,00
260   M = S + 2 * (N + 1):S2 = S + 2
270   D = M - S
280   IF D > 255 THEN 310
290   POKE S2,D: POKE S2 + 1,0
300   GOTO 330
310   D1 =  INT (D / 256):D2 = D - D1 * 256
320   POKE S2,D2: POKE S2 + 1,D1
330   S2 = S2 + 2
340   READ A
350   IF A = 8 THEN 420
360   READ B
370   IF B = 8 THEN 410
380   X = B * 8 + A
390   POKE M,X:M = M + 1
400   GOTO 340
410   POKE M,A:M = M + 1
420   POKE M,0:M = M + 1
430   Q = Q - 1
440   IF Q = 0 THEN  RETURN
450   GOTO 270
```

```
457   REM
458   REM   *** DATA FOR CAR AND MIDDLE LINES ***
459   REM
460   DATA     2
470   DATA 2,2,2,2,2,2,2,2,2,2,2,7,7,7,7,4,4,7,7,6,6,7
      ,7,4,4,4,4,4,4,5,5,6,6,5,5,4,4,4,4,4,4,4,4,4,4,7
      ,7,6,6,7,7,4,4,4,4,4,5,5,6,6,5,5,4,4,4,4,5,5,4
      ,4,5,5
480   DATA   5,5,6,6,5,5,6,6,6,6,5,5,4,4,5,5,6,6,6,6,6,
      6,7,7,4,4,7,7,6,6,6,6,6,6,6,6,6,6,5,5,4,4,5,5,6,6
      ,6,6,6,6,7,7,4,4,7,7,6,6,7,7,7,7
490   DATA   8
500   DATA   4,4,4,4,4,4,4,4,4,4,4,4,4,4,4,8
999   REM
1000  REM   *** MIDDLE LINES ***
1001  REM
1010  XDRAW 2 AT 140,F
1020  XDRAW 2 AT 140,G
1030  XDRAW 2 AT 140,H
1040  XDRAW 2 AT 140,I
1050  XDRAW 2 AT 140,J
1051  RETURN
1057  REM
1058  REM   *** DRAW MOVING MIDDLE LINES & CALCULATE
               NEW POSITION OF LINES ***
1059  REM
1060  XDRAW 2 AT 140,F
1070  XDRAW 2 AT 140,G
1080  XDRAW 2 AT 140,H
1090  XDRAW 2 AT 140,I
1100  XDRAW 2 AT 140,J
1110  F = F + Z:G = G + Z:H = H + Z:I = I + Z
1120  J = J + Z
1130  IF F > 175 THEN F = 1
1140  IF G > 175 THEN G = 1
1150  IF H > 175 THEN H = 1
1160  IF I > 175 THEN I = 1
1170  IF J > 175 THEN J = 1
1180  RETURN
```

```
1999   REM
2000   REM  *** SCRAPING SIDE ***
2001   REM
2010   CL = PEEK ( - 16336) +  PEEK ( - 16336) - PEEK
       ( - 16336) + PEEK ( - 16336)
2020   RETURN
2999   REM
3000   REM  *** CRASH - END GAME ***
3001   REM
3010   XDRAW 1 AT X,Y
3020   END
```

Joystick Calibration

```
        JOYSTICK CALIBRATION
   Horizontal and Vertical Adjustment
---------------------------------------



        Aligned if  H=127  V=127
            VERTICAL = 127
          HORIZONTAL = 127







 (C)ontinue, or SPACE to Recheck...
```

Games were a big part of my life thanks to my Apple II and a joystick was an essential part of gameplay. While I started with Apple's classic joystick with orange buttons and a black handle, I eventually graduated to a CH Products Mach III joystick with an extra button on top. Now that's fun!

Naturally, I wanted to make sure my entertainment device was properly calibrated. Thus, this program starts by checking the horizontal and vertical alignment, then tests button #0 and #1.

```
1  REM  * JOYSTICK CALIBRATION *
2  REM  **** BY BRIAN WISER ****
3  REM
4  REM
8  TEXT : HOME : NORMAL : HTAB 11: PRINT "JOYSTICK
   CALIBRATION"
```

```
10   VTAB 3: PRINT "  Horizontal and Vertical
     Adjustment   ": PRINT " -------------------------
     -----------": PRINT
15   VTAB 10: HTAB 9: PRINT "Aligned if  H=127  V=127"
20   VTAB 12: PRINT "                 VERTICAL = ";:
     INVERSE : PRINT  PDL (1);: NORMAL : PRINT " ":
     PRINT "               HORIZONTAL = ";:
25   INVERSE : PRINT  PDL (0);: NORMAL : PRINT " ":A =
     PDL (1):B =  PDL (0): IF A > 126 AND A < 128 AND
     B > 126 AND B < 128 THEN 40
30   FOR C = 1 TO 10: NEXT C: GOTO 20
40   VTAB 24: PRINT "(C)ontinue, or SPACE to
     Recheck...";: GET A$: IF A$ = "C" OR A$ = "c" THEN
     60
50   IF A$ =  CHR$ (32) THEN 8
60   HOME
70   VTAB 5: HTAB 10: PRINT "Press LEFT Button #0": IF
     PEEK ( - 16287) < 128 THEN 70
80   PRINT : INVERSE : HTAB 10: PRINT "LEFT Button #0
     Okay": NORMAL
90   VTAB 11: HTAB 10: PRINT "Press RIGHT Button #1":
     IF  PEEK ( - 16286) < 128 THEN 90
100  PRINT : INVERSE : HTAB 10: PRINT "RIGHT Button
     #1 Okay": NORMAL : PRINT : PRINT : HTAB 8: PRINT
     "Joystick Ready For Use": PRINT
```

www.ingramcontent.com/pod-product-compliance
Lightning Source LLC
Chambersburg PA
CBHW041104180526
45172CB00001B/97

* 9 7 8 1 3 8 7 8 1 8 5 8 7 *